Beat the Goatskin till the Goat Cries

Notes from a Kerry Village

For Kris and Lisa Kristofferson

GABRIEL FITZMAURICE

Beat the Goatskin till the Goat Cries

Notes from a Kerry Village

Many thanks —

Gabriel Fitzmaurice

MERCIER PRESS

WHAT YOU NEED TO READ

MERCIER PRESS
Douglas Village, Cork
www.mercierpress.ie

Trade enquiries to Columba Mercier Distribution,
55a Spruce Avenue, Stillorgan Industrial Park, Blackrock, Dublin

1 85635 500 4

10 9 8 7 6 5 4 3 2 1

Mercier Press receives financial assistance from
the Arts Council/An Chomhairle Ealaíon

Printed and Bound by ColourBooks Ltd

CONTENTS

A Kerry of the Mind

It has become a commonplace to say that a given place is a state of mind. And yet, this is true of many places – of any place whose people re-create themselves in their environment. Kerry is such a place. We have been fed romantic, Celtic-twilight images of Kerry by the tourist industry with such success that not only do tourists flock to Kerry, but the natives half believe the soft focus, tinted images of their lives too.

What sort of place is Kerry? Look to the landscape – ocean, river, lake, mountain, hill, bog, pasture and plain. Some believe that a landscape explains a people, defines them. I don't know. But I *do* know that landscape influences people – who cannot but be influenced by breakers in a gale charging the cliffs in Clochar or Ballybunion?; who cannot but be pared down to bare essentials by the mountains of Corca Dhuibhne or Uíbh Ráthach?; who cannot but be awed by a stippled sunset over Cnoc an Fhómhair, or a silver moon tinselling a bog in Sliabh Luachra or Oidhreacht Uí Chonchubhair? Indeed! But what defines us is our language. We are what we can say.

Kerry has two languages, *Gaeilge* and English. The landscape is named in bastard English – a nonsense concocted from the original Irish by map makers for the Ordnance Survey in the nineteenth century. In their original form, the place names 'said' their landscape, translated it for its people. Kerry was *Ciarraighe*, 'the territory of the people of Ciar', the son of Fergus Mac Roighe and Queen Maeve of Connacht. The name 'Kerry' is, of itself, meaningless. Yet, 'Kerry' now means what it says: though lacking the historical and cultural resonances of *Ciarraighe*, it means today the place and its people.

Who are the Kerry people? John B. Keane has described the Kerryman as 'the Greater, Hard-necked Atlantic Warbler … who quests individually and in flocks for all forms of diversion and is to be found high and low, winter and summer, wherever there is the remotest prospect of drink, sex, confusion or commotion'! And that, indeed, is how many Kerry people are perceived. There is a larger-than-life, hyperbolic dimension to Kerry people. Cute and canny as we are, we seem to revel in living our lives in public – perhaps this is why, as a county, we have produced so many storytellers, singers, writers, footballers and talkers who *need* to perform in public. It is as if the closed, secretive atmosphere of the small village – and Kerry is full of small villages – explodes and displays all in public, like the person who won't confess privately to the priest, baring all to the nation on the radio or television.

I get the profound feeling that Kerry people need to express themselves, and will do so no matter what. And Kerry people like to hear about themselves. They flock to local 'theatres' – parish halls, community centres – to see the latest John B. Keane play, curious to see themselves on stage. They make the required objections to the 'vulgarity' of the language (knowing that 'vulgar' means 'of the common people', i.e. themselves!), but are secretly delighted for they know that all is truth, that we are everything that happens; they see themselves reflected in the play.

Kerry people are inquisitive – 'curious' is the way we say it here. They like to meet strangers, to find out about them, to talk to them. Many strangers, indeed, have put down roots among us and have become more Kerry than Kerry itself! For Kerry

8

people, I feel, welcome outsiders among them. They enjoy the exotic, the foreign, the fantastic and the fabulous. It must be remembered that we are now only one generation removed from being believers in the otherworld of the *sidhe,* the *piseog,* a magic world full of the possibility of good and evil. Scratch a Kerryman, even today, and you will find a superstitious streak. The vast majority of Kerry people still practise their religion – in most cases, the Roman Catholic faith, some Church of Ireland, and, recently, some Jehovah's Witnesses who are making inroads in the heretofore conservative and traditional field of religious practice. Kerry Catholics, like most Irish Catholics, are partly pagan, and some of their traditional practices, patterns, holy wells, etc. date back to pre-Christian Ireland. Unfortunately, the Protestant community is dwindling, many of their churches closed and converted to arts centres, heritage centres and so on.

Kerry people have traditionally lived off the land – farmers for the most part, part-time fishermen, some-time labourers (anything to supplement the family income). The land varies in quality from rich arable land to poor, hungry land making life difficult for the subsistence farmer. It is no wonder, then, that Kerry has produced so many teachers, nuns, priests and brothers: that was the traditional way to improve one's station in life, though there is a well documented love of learning in the area as well. As early as 1672, Sir William Petty noted that 'the French and Latin tongues' were known 'amongst the poorest Irish and chiefly in Kerry, most remote from Dublin.' On 27 May 1673 the 'Report of Lord Herbert, John Butler and Cadogan Barnes, Justices of the county of Kerry' commented that 'the said County aboundeth … with youth learning of needless Latin instead of useful trades'. Some twenty years later, George Story, chaplain to Gower's regiment in the Williamite forces in Ireland, remarked that 'every cow-boy amongst them (i.e. Kerry people) can speak Latin, on purpose to save them from the Gallows, when they come afterwards to be tried for Theft!'

But all is truth, as I have said, and there is another side to the story. We all have read of cases like *The Kerry Babies* where infants are found dead in wells and on beaches; there is violence and crime (not as widespread as elsewhere, but nonetheless significant); and there is unemployment. Uíbh Ráthach (I prefer the original to 'Iveragh' or 'South Kerry') is severely disabled by unemployment and its consequent emigration. Other areas too. Parishes that could field a football team twenty years ago cannot now do so – unless father togs out with son to make up fifteen. *Something will have to be done* is the cry from parish pump to parliament. And soon, before it is too late and our most beautiful landscape becomes a playground for the rich, the privileged, the foreigner and the speculator.

In compiling a book called *Kerry Through its Writers* in 1993, I was interested to hear what native Kerry men and women, and adopted Kerry men and women, had to say. I was curious to hear how they would respond to Kerry. I left theme and tone open to individual utterance – how he/she responded to life in Kerry, how he/she related to it, how he/she defined, and was defined by, it. The responses were various and vibrant. I learned more about Kerry, and ultimately about myself, from reading their contributions – no man is an island, and there is a sense that one is not simply *of* a county but that the county becomes one, that people are place and place is people. We have called up Kerry in language. Kerry exists in language, the song line of its people.

2

Culpable Innocence?

Rural life is under threat. More particularly, life in the west of Ireland is under threat. From without. From within. It is under threat from without by the images it has foisted upon it – images of itself in another's narrative, images of itself in poor circumstances compared with images of easy affluence, of sex-'n'-drugs-'n'-rock-'n'-roll in foreign parts: 'Faraway cows have long horns, and faraway fields are green'. It is under threat economically. It is under resourced, under funded, under developed. Misunderstood.

Culchies and *Kerrymen* are the butt of bad jokes. These jokes are told, it is said, in good part, and are taken, it is said, in good part. Indeed, we Culchies and Kerrymen sometimes tell these jokes against ourselves. But it is a form of discrimination – much akin to the anti male ads, depicting men as nincompoops or morons, on television. No one today would dare employ such images of women. But it sells soap powders and washing-up liquid, much as *Kerryman* jokes sell books. The *Culchie* and *Kerryman* jokes are no less objectionable. They trivialise not just Culchies and Kerrymen, but all rural life. It is a measure of our confidence that we have shrugged off this patronising, this discrimination, this deliberate misrepresentation, this false image.

Rural life is under threat also from within. It is under threat from poor self image, from hopelessness, from depression, from unemployment. And every society has its gombeens who abuse their own people for financial gain, or to gain in power, in influence, in prestige. I have always been inclined to consign these people to the ignominy where they belong. It has been suggested to me that this is a kind of culpable innocence. But a person can only dominate as permitted. It is not a case of the ostrich in the sand; not a case of ignore-it-and-it-will-disappear. It is always with us. I, and many who live in the west, have chosen to make it irrelevant. How? By a process of re-creation.

Re-creation. Not recreation as escape, as pastime, as hobby, but re-creation as a re-creating of ourselves in our communities, thus transforming our environment – emotional, cultural, spiritual. Éamon de Valera had an early version, much maligned today by everyone from popstars to politicians. I would not, or could not, malign it, except to point to its 'culpable innocence'. His comely maidens (and young men) dancing at the crossroads, or nowadays at the disco, in the dance hall (if such a phenomenon exists any more!), in the community centre, in the pub, in their minds – wherever, but dancing – is not what this country needs economically, but it is a vital part of the spiritual well-being of its people. We might be down, but we're not out. We transport ourselves in music, in song, dance, sport, in art, in literature. Even destitute, there are those among us who live life to the full. Such a man was Willie Dore, a friend and neighbour of mine in the village. I have written his story in verse:

Willie Dore was simple,
He smelled. The village fool,
He lived alone among the rats
In a shack below the school.

Two rats' eyes in his leather face
Stabbed out beneath the layer

Of dirt that blackened him like soot.
He wasn't born *quare*,

But some disease the doctor
Couldn't cure (or name)
Trapped him in his childhood
Hobbling his brain.

Willie Dore was a happy man
Though peevish as a huff –
He fed, he drank, he slept, he rose,
He dreamed – that was enough …

Each sausage scrounged from a travelling van
Was a vital victory;
Each penny coaxed from a passing priest
Was a cunning comedy.

Willie never knew his age –
No matter how you'd pry,
'The one age to Mary Mack'
Was all he could reply.

He lived as he imagined,
Saw manna in the street,
Eighty years of scavenging,
Admitting no defeat.

We transform ourselves in ritual: in rituals of our Church ('Oh
death, where is thy sting-a-ling-a-ling? Or grave thy victory?');
in rituals we develop ourselves. In developing our own rituals,
we exist in our own mythology. 'Mythology' or 'myth' should

not be used as a synonym for 'lie' or 'untruth'. A myth is the symbolic manifestation of a psychological truth. By our myths you know us. A people without a myth is a poor people. They are the real poor.

A small community such as my own is as close as the late twentieth century can get to a classless society. Sure! there are economic divisions. Sure! there are people who consider themselves superior to their neighbours, and who look down on them. But look at the parish football team. You can't buy your way on to that. You can't 'pull' yourself into it. Look at the local Wrenboys. To the democracy of talent. If you, man, woman or child, can sing, make music, dance, play the fool, tell stories or recite, you'll get your place. And no matter what your social status, no matter what your bank balance, if you're a good sports person, musician, actor, dancer or whatever – if you're good, you are respected. Nor does the class system obtain in the parish schools. All the tots-to-twelves in the parish attend the parish schools. Again, the pitch is level. The children vary as to ability intellectually, artistically, musically, athletically, but *who* they are won't make them *what* they are.

Let us look again at the Wrenboys, the revellers of Christmas and Saint Stephen's Day. It has been suggested that they are 'vagabonds and vagrants'. Shame! Sure, they collect money. In these politically correct times, some collect now for charity, or for community projects; some, God bless them, still blow the money on wild 'Wren Parties' with friends and neighbours (i.e. the very people they collected the money from in the first place); some go on the Wren to defray the costs of Christmas, a Christmas that gets more expensive by the year as kids are bombarded by ads on television and radio, by fliers from toy sellers, etc. But to the Wren itself. Some people will lock out these revellers. More lock them in. I know of houses where the woman of the house will lock in the Wrenboys so that the household will have an extra period of revelry at the worst time of the year. Like Eliot's Magi, the Wrenboys have a cold coming of it. Anyone who was ever on the Wren, and I have been a Wrenboy, will tell you that it's worse than a day in the bog, or a day in the meadow. Whatever they get wouldn't pay them. For they bring Christmas with them; they bring tradition; fabulously mortal, they bring revelry and exuberance and not a little madness. And we need this exuberance, this madness, we need this festival at the worst time of the year. December 25th was the Roman feast of *natalis invicti*, the birth of light, of that which could not be destroyed. The Wrenboys know this instinctively. The year, and we, are at our lowest ebb. The Wrenboys celebrate the birth of light. They walk in their own mythology; they celebrate for all. There is something profoundly pagan in this. But what is a 'pagan'? Through its Latin root, *paganus*, it is a village dweller. When the enlightenment (i.e. the new religion, Christianity) hit the Roman empire, it took off in the cities first; the *pagani* (the Culchies, the Kerrymen!) remained with the old faith. I am not in any sense suggesting anything profane when I say that the Wrenboys are pagan – they are villagers following old ways, old customs.

And so, the community re-creates itself – in Church, in pubs, in kitchens, in community centres, in sports fields, in parish halls, in its own mind. Mostly, we make our own entertainment, we create our own narratives. The alternative is to be entertained – to be passive (or critical) consumers of other's narratives. It is a fragile balance, but one which allows us to thrive in an often hostile world.

'Ring out the Old, Ring in the New'

Customs are important, not so much because they preserve the past as that they keep it alive. I am no fanatical conservationist – the past holds no preservation order over me – but I want to let the past live in me. We cannot live in the past, but the past can live in us. That is why I like to see old customs passed on.

So we ring out the old year. Or, at least we used to. I remember ringing out the old year about 1970 in Moyvane. I would have been about eighteen years old and in leaving certificate year in secondary school. I was determined to go out on the street to ring out the old, ring in the new. I could persuade nobody to join me. All my friends were going to dances in the neighbouring towns. They abandoned me to my scheme. In those years, the pubs closed before midnight. The drinkers dispersed. I had almost given up when a friend of mine, a university student, emerged from some corner of the village. He had a mouth organ. So had I. We stood in the centre of the deserted village and blew and sucked music from our humble instruments.

Tennyson was on my leaving cert. course so I stood at Brosnan's Corner and recited at the top of my voice:

Ring out, wild bells, to the wild sky,
The flying cloud, the frosty night:
The year is dying in the night;
Ring out, wild bells, and let him die.

Ring out the old, ring in the new,
Ring, happy bells, across the snow;
The year is going, let him go …

Sometime about one o'clock, we called it a night. The following morning as I strolled out, the villagers (at least those who couldn't sleep because of our midnight ceremony) were annoyed. Was the custom dead?

Twenty-something years later, Maurice Heffernan, then chairman of the local Wrenboy group, and I decided to revive the custom. He could let us have the Wrenboys' torches (metal containers mounted on wooden polls in which were held blazing sods of turf soaked in diesel); he could organise musicians. Could I organise the crowd? First things first – musicians and torch bearers were organised. Gathering a crowd was a different matter. When I asked some teenagers if they'd like to ring out the old year, they looked puzzled and asked me what it was. Yes! It had come to that.

It was midnight. The musicians assembled – banjo, tin-whistle, accordion, mandoline and bodhrán. The torch bearers lit their torches and raised them up into the night. Carrying our own light, we marched through the village. Through the open doors of midnight, drinkers spilled from pubs. We marched up and down the village and halted at the cross where we played and danced, wished each other a happy new year and sang 'Auld Lang Syne' before we dispersed. In the following years the practice declined. Bad weather, absent musicians, lack of enthusiasm contributed.

But I, or anyone who saw it, will never forget that first night when the village marched through the doors of midnight into a new year, singing, dancing, making music, carrying its own light, the seed of which might fire a youngster's imagination in years to come to revive the past again.

My Own Place

Like a dog and its master,
Like a ship on the water,
I need you, you bitch,
Newtown.
I need you, you bitch,
Newtown.

Thus ends a poem I wrote many years ago about my native place. The poem was called 'Lovers'. When questioned (in the pub – where else?!) about the title, I replied rather cockily, 'Love is a conflict'. I suppose I meant by that, that when two interests clash, there is an inevitable conflict.

The sentiments expressed in the above poem are very much a young man's sentiments. A young man facing up to the consequences of his choices. I had chosen to live in 'Newtown' in 1975, believing it to be still the village of my childhood. Nowhere ever is – I found that out pretty quickly! I should, of course, have learned that lesson in leaving cert. Máirtín Ó Direáin, returning to his native Inishmore, laments:

Mé ar thóir m'óige ar bealach,
Mé im' Oisín ar na craga,
Is fós ar fud an chladaigh,
Mé ag caoineadh slua na marbh.

(I seek my youth on the road,
I am Oisín on the crags
Wandering on the strand
Lamenting the hosts of the dead.)

But I didn't learn from Ó Direáin in leaving cert. Youth seldom learns from other's experience – youth will risk experience of its own. And so, having qualified as a national teacher in 1972; having taught in Avoca, Co. Wicklow and in Limerick City, I chose to return to the village of my childhood to take up a teaching post in 1975. I have lived here ever since.

The village of my childhood was Newtown Sandes, so named after the landlord's agents, the much hated Sandes family. As far back as 1886, the locals sought to change the name. After a public meeting in the village, the citizenry agreed henceforth to call the village 'Newtown Dillon' – for John Dillon, the MP who was involved in the national and land struggles at that time. (He attended that particular meeting in the village.) But habits are hard to change and, little by little, people forgot about 'Newtown Dillon', preferring the familiar 'Newtown Sandes' instead. In 1916, the name was changed to 'Newtown Clarke' for Thomas Clarke, one of the executed leaders of the Easter Rising. 'Newtown Clarke' suffered a similar fate to 'Newtown Dillon'. In 1939, a move was made to have the name officially changed to 'Moyvane' ('The Middle Plain'), the name of the townland on which the village is situated. Eventually, in the late 1960s, the name was (semi) officially changed to 'Moyvane', though for years afterwards one could still see 'Newtown Sandes' on road signs! (This created terrible confusion. I remember being accosted by an irate and confused lorry driver looking for 'Newtown Sandes Co-op' who had followed 'Newtown Sandes' on the road signs only to end up in 'Moyvane'!) Some of the more popular road maps still carry the

19

name 'Newtown Sandes', which adds to the confusion.

Moyvane is a small, sleepy straggle of a village about seven miles from Listowel in north Kerry, and off the main road – so much off the main road that one could say that life, like the traffic, is passing us by. Most parishioners have cars which they use increasingly to transport them out of Moyvane for shopping, for business, and for entertainment. There is a sense that the car, like the telephone, is keeping the people in touch with the life that is passing them by. As the son of a small shopkeeper who earned his living in Moyvane, I have mixed feelings about this rush to the supermarkets. The local shop epitomised the community. One shopped in the local shops and more often than not, one got much needed credit until the creamery cheque was cashed, or one drew the pension or the dole. That same shop was a place to congregate, to ruminate and to spread the news. It had an important social function. But times have changed. One simply cannot live in the past. All the same, I have my doubts about the supermarket mentality: the supermarket mentality stands for consumerism and anonymity, neither of which greatly appeals to me.

Derelict buildings in the village are being pulled down. There are still more that need to be pulled down. Old people dying, leaving old houses which soon become derelict. Children break the windows by throwing stones. (Hard to blame them – such windows weren't too safe when we were kids, either!). Old people dying. The young getting out. The story, not just of this village, but of the whole of rural Ireland. Why would anyone want to remain?

I suppose it's fair to say that most of the people who live in Moyvane were either born here or have married into the parish. If one can resist the bright lights of places far away ('faraway cows have long horns'!), and if one can earn a living here,

Moyvane is a very good place to be. The pace of life is as slow and easy as the cattle that amble through the village, morning and evening, to the milking parlours in the village farmyards. One doesn't have to develop a paranoia about locking things up: if you forget to lock the house at night, the chances are it won't be burgled; if you forget to lock the car, it's unlikely 'twill be stolen. The people are a gay and friendly people who are passionate about sport – the traditional passions are for football and greyhounds, but now the younger generation are excelling at basketball and badminton, athletics too. The pubs are convivial and, at times, boisterous with hilarity and song.

In villages such as Moyvane, the old adage rings true: 'ar scáth a chéile a mhaireann na daoine' ('people depend on each other') for people *do* help one another and are concerned for one another. If, on occasion, this concern is carried over, by misguided busybodies, to prying, I still wouldn't or couldn't describe Moyvane as a Valley of Squinting Windows.

Curiously, in such an arable countryside, there are no Protestants among our farming folk. There are no Protestants – full stop. There is no Protestant church, nor the remains of one, in the parish. There are two modern Roman Catholic churches in the parish – one in Moyvane village, described by Barrington, in *Discovering Kerry*, as 'of an ugliness indescribable'! The other, in Knockanure village contains, among many beautiful contemporary works of art, a carving of The Last Supper by Oisín Kelly.

Yes! Moyvane is my own place. If I have mixed feelings about it – well, I have mixed feelings about myself! There are advantages and disadvantages to living here. But that is true of everywhere. In the final analysis, the best I can say is that I am happy here. I don't suppose I would write 'I need you, you bitch, Newtown' now. But the best love is never based on need. Love is based on giving and I would give Moyvane anything I have to give.

A Kerry Joke

On the periphery of Ireland, on the periphery of Europe, we stand alone, the butt of bureaucrats and bad jokes. Abandoned to our own resources, we are cast upon ourselves.

A region of abandoned homesteads and unprofitable farms, we look to the future mindful of the past. How many lovely villages of the plain will be deserted before the Eurocrats call 'Enough'? How many village schoolmasters must lock up their schools before they call 'Enough'? Are we doomed, as Goldsmith's peasants were in the 1770s, to live in a region of deserted villages where 'rural mirth and manners are no more'?

'We learn from history that we learn nothing from history' George Bernard Shaw has warned us. Alas, it seems we have learned nothing except that the winner takes all. Losers lose well. It's an endearing trait. The gracious in defeat will not inherit the earth. No! They will forever be minions in a victors' world, invisible, voiceless and without rights. They are the local colour in the global map. The maps, like the histories, are drawn up by the victors.

So we are Kerry people. Ah sure, you know us – Kerrymen jokes, the 'Paddies' of Ireland who know how to laugh at ourselves when others mock us, whose silence is our last resort. By our silence you know us. Through it, we ingratiate ourselves. Through it, we outwit our 'betters'. Through it, we betray ourselves. That is the price of silence.

We are silent because we have been defeated. Our history is

a history of defeat. A colonised people, we are still struggling with the consequences of our history. In a post colonial state we are reluctant to break free from the comforts (the constraints) of our history and to face the challenge of freedom with all its uncertainty and risk. That is the price of defeat. It is also the price of freedom.

We must refuse to be minor characters in someone else's story. We must create our own story. On the highways and the byways, in our kitchens and in our pubs, in our football fields, our theatres and churches, we must say ourselves, we must play ourselves, we must pray ourselves. Until we have a clear vision of, and for, ourselves we must refuse to see ourselves as others see us. We must stop apologising for ourselves. We must acknowledge our individuality, our uniqueness within the framework of our community.

Where are the leaders of our community now? Where is our voice in Europe? Jackie Healy-Rae spoke up for his people. He was ridiculed for being a Kerryman, for his brogue, for his bravado. Even those who gave him a hearing made him into a sort of Clown Prince of Kerry. The old syndrome – the Kerry joke – personified in Healy-Rae. But he spoke up, powerfully and unafraid. We await the other, more urbane, voices to advocate our cause. To stand up and be counted. In the name of Kerry. In the name of justice.

Oliver Cromwell drove the native Irish westwards – to hell or to Connacht (which also included Clare). We, the people of Clare and Kerry, are still living in these regions. Parliament (our own, and in Europe) marginalises us. It's as if they wished we'd go away. Then greed could buy up the homesteads and the farmsteads, as our homely, people-friendly townlands and villages sell up, and are converted into impersonal, but profitable, units of production. But no man is an island, as the poet John

Donne wrote nearly 400 years ago. He was concerned about our interdependence. Not just individuals. As individuals are interdependent, as communities are interdependent, so too are counties, countries and even continents. 'Every man' Donne warns us, 'is a peece of the *Continent*, a part of the *maine*; if a *Clod* bee washed away by the *Sea*, *Europe* is the less, as well as if a *Promontorie* were, as well as if a *Mannor* of thy *friends* or of *thine own* were; any mans *death* diminishes *me*, because I am involved in *Mankinde*; And therefore never send to know for whom the *bell* tolls; It tolls for *thee.*'

If the bell is not to toll for Europe, it would do well to remember places like Kerry and Clare, and how every clod washed from Slea Head or Loop Head has infinite consequences not just for Europe, but for the whole of mankind. People are place, and place is people. Every abandoned farm, every deserted village calls out for justice. Every abandoned farm, every deserted village accuses those who stood idly by while bureaucrats bargained and sold. They will not be easily forgiven.

Home

Home is where the heart is. Maybe. But also where the head is. Christ said of Himself that the Son of Man had no place to lay His head. Maybe that's what home is: the place you can lay your head – in rest, in reverie; the place where you are reconciled to yourself and your environment, emotional, physical, spiritual. A little bit of heaven, so to speak.

Home for me is Moyvane, Co. Kerry. More particularly, it is the house where I live; the place I love; the place I write, make music and dream. There's nothing I like better than to take a guitar out to the garden and play until I am in tune, at one, with myself, with my surroundings, both in harmony and in praise. To be *at one* is, in a special sense, to *atone.* So here I am in my garden *at-one-ing,* making peace – with myself, with my environment. Larks sing overhead, bees buzz in the flowers, cows in the nearby fields convert grass to milk. Here I am filled with the milk of human kindness. This, for me, is home.

OK. Not everybody feels this way about home. If home for me is heaven, home for some is hell. Or a place to get out of, and fast. Even so, don't we define ourselves in relation to home? Not just to our own homes, but to an abstract, even ideal, sense of *home.* How often have we heard of the effects of home on everyone from Elvis to Eichmann, from criminals to crime busters. Alas, there is a sense in which home always fails us. It has been said that the difference between an Englishman and an Irishman is that home for an Englishman is his castle, for an Irishman, his prison! Whether home is a castle or a prison, we're not content.

Alexander Pope (1688–1722) wrote:

Happy the man whose wish and care
A few paternal acres bound,
Content to breathe his native air
In his own ground.

Admittedly, he was only about twelve years old when he wrote those lines, but there's something not quite right about this contentment. Contentment is wealth as the saying goes. But wealth can be spent in every sense of the word. Deep down in us there's something that is never content, that can never be satisfied. Saint Augustine tells us that this is our yearning for God. *Thou hast made us for Thyself, O Lord, and our hearts are ever restless until they rest in Thee*, he prayed. So home is a reflection of the eternal longing in all of us. Maybe this is why the Son of Man could find no place to lay His head. He, more than any, knew this eternal longing, and He knew that this world would not satisfy it.

'Property is theft', Karl Marx pronounced in the nineteenth century. He was, of course, condemning capitalism. It has often struck me how close communism as an ideal is to Christ (if not always to Christianity). Particularly in relation to property. As easy for a camel to pass through the eye of a needle as for a rich man to enter the kingdom of heaven.

Breathing my native air in my own ground, I can only offer my thanks for the goodness life has brought me. On his eviction from the Garden of Paradise, Adam was enjoined to earn his bread by the sweat of his brow. Eventually we would come to realise, in the words of the Latin proverb *(laborare est orare)*, that

26

```
             Shane's
        401 Lighthouse Ave.
         Monterey, Ca 93940
           (831) 646-2005


Server: Shane              Station: 2

Order #: 12889              Dine In
Table: d                   Guests: 1


1 LUNCH IRISH STEW            9.00
1 GUINNESS                    5.00

Bar Subtotal:                5.00
Food Subtotal:               9.00
Add on Tax:                  0.65
                          ----------
AMOUNT DUE:                $14.65

          >> Ticket #: 7 <<
        6/1/2008 8:26:44 PM


             THANK YOU!
```

to work is to pray. Far from being an act of theft, my property, my garden of paradise, is the fruit of my labour, bought with the sweat of my brow. When Karl Marx declared that property was theft, he was mercifully unaware of the modern house mortgage! A modern Karl Marx might observe that property, far from being theft, is a form of slavery. Amen to that!

Sunday Night in Máiréad's Bar, Moyvane

In Ireland we have a worrying ambivalence about drinking. We have statues to Father Matthew, Pioneer Total Abstinence rallies, accusations that adult drinking leads to teenage substance abuse and so on. Like any citizen, I worry about these things. But, you know, because the Last Supper couldn't have happened without wine, I think there is a sacrament of drinking.

To go into a local pub (we're not talking about yuppie drinking emporia here), to sit down in company with the neighbours, to join them over a few pints, to meet, perchance to sing, is, as a preacher might pronounce (if he could divest himself of his inhibitions), a kind of sacrament. I've been in pubs where people discover themselves in such communion. Take the regular drinker who would die rather than call attention to himself but who, in the conviviality of the occasion, takes up a bodhrán and keeps time with the music. To the cultured, or even the casual, ear his 'playing' is an abomination, dominating, destroying the music. Maybe so. But we country folk weren't reared with the bodhrán – we were reared with 'tambourines' – great, noisy goatskin drums that, unlike the bodhrán, had the flattened tops of beer bottles inserted into the rim the more to jingle-jangle in revelry with the music. These tambourines were meant to be played outdoors on the 'Wren', the Bacchanalia of Saint Stephen's Day, when large batches of musicians and revellers went out 'on the Wren', making music, making merry, visiting house to house from townland to townland bringing Christmas, bringing solstice. If the more refined bodhrán is the preferred instrument of the concert stage (and it is more sympathetic to the sensitivities of the virtuoso), we remember the 'Wren' where one beat the goatskin 'till the goat cried'.

And so tonight, I dropped into my local for a pint. It's the kind of pub that's friendly to characters, to the unusual, the offbeat, the eccentric. In I went to find John Willis, a box player from Athea, the next parish, and Mike Chawke, a fiddler from Ballyhahill, also over the border in west Limerick, in full flight, Willis in his Nike baseball cap, fag drooping over a greying beard, Chawke with his left heel resting on his right ankle transporting themselves, and us, into the dimension of the heart. Inevitably, they were joined by a bodhrán player, a drummer of the old style – Pat Mulvihill who punched that goatskin, revealing himself in its primal beat. There are players who are note perfect, there are players whose virtuosity would mesmerise you, but this is the land of the heart. It's hearty music we want tonight. And this is what we get. When I complemented John Willis, the fag still drooping from his lips, he smiled at me and said: 'Gabriel, we're keeping ourselves warm for the winter.'

In the pulse of their music, we feel our own pulse. The music inspires us. And we inspire the music until we are literally breathing the music, players and audience becoming one in the joy of our shared experience. In the communion of drinkers, in the sacrament of beer.

(Written in 2000)

8

Corner Boys

Much has been written, and said, about corner boys. They are disparaged as a species, looked down upon and maligned as a group. They are said, by people who have never spent a morning in their company, to be wasters, good-for-nothings, idlers, spongers, even a threat to society. I have been a corner boy. I am proud to admit it. I would dearly love to spend more time with the poets and philosophers of the street corner.

When I was studying for my leaving certificate, one of the prescribed essays was 'An Apology for Idlers' by Robert Louis Stevenson. (Instead of being *prescribed*, I'm surprised it wasn't *proscribed* because of its potential effect on minds like mine.) What I remember most about that essay was that Stevenson believed that idling was a creative endeavour – hardly a pastime at all. And that is how I view the occupation of my friends the corner boys.

Wordsworth admonished us that the world is too much with us, that in getting and spending we lay waste our powers. Milton taught us that they also serve who only stand and wait. Those are lessons we can learn at the street corner. Away from the getting and spending of the workaday world, the corner boys have learned to stand and wait. They cast a bemused eye on our headlong rush for profit. God will provide. (Yes, I know, dear tax payer, that the tax payer provides – I'm a tax payer too. But where would any of us be without God?).

Corner boys have learned to make do with less. They are

happy in their own company. They are happy to share that company with others who have a genuine interest in their culture.

To spend a Saturday morning laughing and joking at the corner is to get the world in perspective, is to see that maybe, after all, God's in his heaven and all's right with the world.

In the Sermon on the Mount, Jesus asks which of us by taking thought can add one cubit to his stature? 'Consider the lilies of the field,' he reminds us, 'how they grow, they toil not, neither do they spin.' And yet our heavenly Father takes care of them. Like the corner boys, we would do well to 'take no thought for the morrow: for the morrow shall take thought for the things of itself. Sufficient unto the day,' Jesus tells us, 'is the evil thereof.'

A CORNER BOY

Just lazing at the cross with friends and neighbours,
Just gossiping the morning hours away
Returning to the time when we, teenagers,
Learned to stand and wait, an idle day
When dogs curled up and slept at Brosnan's Corner,
When our lives stretched out before us like a haze,
When everything seemed happier and warmer –
Ah yes! Those were the very best of days.
And here I am again at Brosnan's Corner
Gossiping the morning hours away.
No! The past was neither happier nor warmer –
Sufficient is its evil to the day.
I stand here with my back against the wall,
Take no thought for a world in its own thrall.

9

Christmas

Christmas has always fascinated me. By its magic. By its mystery. But especially by its loneliness. I don't mean loneliness in a morbid or misanthropic sense. I mean that I've always felt especially alone at Christmas.

It's a time to look in as much as to look out. I suppose my being an only child has much to do with this. An only child spends much time alone – there are no brothers or sisters at home to play, or even fight, with. So you fall back on yourself a lot. You live in your imagination a lot. You spend a lot of time with adults, particularly your parents.

So my Christmas is a Christmas of the imagination, spent in my own company and in the company of adults. Particularly on Christmas Day. Mammy, Daddy and I would sit down to the turkey and trimmings (which my father cooked – my mother had heart trouble, and was often confined to bed); they'd have a glass of sherry with the meal, and I always managed to make enough of a nuisance of myself to ensure that I got a drop, too!

That was the loneliest day – a day spent almost entirely *en famille*, with no friends to play with. This was before television, before video games. So I'd play with my toys or read a book, or just listen to my parents talking. Loneliness was friendly. I could live with it.

I remember one particular Christmas morning, though, when the loneliness got the better of me. Santa had brought me a toy wooden piano. Big enough to play a tune on, but small enough to transport in my arms. Boy! was I excited. I played it and played it from the crack of dawn until I simply couldn't contain myself any longer and burst out of doors in search of an audience. Where could I find one? Where would I be heard? In the church, of course! I tore off to the church where all the people had gathered for mass, and was just about to give a recital in the porch when my father caught up with me and marched me back home – if not to the sound of silence, then to the sound of being alone.

But the following day was Saint Stephen's Day, the day of the Wren! A day of madness and revelry. Santa often brought me a mouth organ – a 'Sonny Boy' or a 'Hero' always in the key of C (such details meant nothing to me then). Of course I couldn't play it, but what matter! I could blow it and suck it, making my own noise, and call to every house in the village collecting pennies. The money meant nothing. The performing everything. Later I would ask my older cousin, Moss Cunningham, to teach me the mouth organ. He had taught himself to play it. He informed me, quite sincerely, that you didn't *learn* the mouth organ – you just picked it up. And so, little by little, I learned to sound *doh, ray, mi*. From there 'twas a short step to playing the local Wren tunes – marches like 'Roddy McCorley', 'The Dawning of the Day', 'O'Neill's', 'O'Rahilly's', 'Thomas Ashe's'. Lovely, simple tunes that stirred the blood.

To this day, although I do not now go out on the Wren, I can barely contain myself on Stephen's Day. The sound of the tambourines, as we used to call them, wakens something wild and reckless in me. I prowl about the house all day trying to divert myself. That night, I become a Wrenboy again, in a manner of speaking: I join Paddy Fitzmaurice, Maurice Heffernan and the other Wrenboys, usually in Máiréad Kearney's pub in the village, and play (I've since graduated to the mandoline and guitar) and sing my heart out until 'time' is called.

But the thing I remember most about Christmas is its mystery. Simple things like going up into the attic to bring down the Christmas ornaments and the crib. It was like leaving the sure and firm earth and ascending into wonder. The attic was full of surprises – things half forgotten were discovered up there; you never quite knew what you'd find. But you always found something. Even now, I get that feeling going up into the attic for Christmas.

A few weeks ago, it came forcefully to me again. John and Nessa, our two children, saw me about to go up into the attic to bring down the Christmas decorations and the crib. Now, Christmas is all about children, and unless we suffer the children to come to us, unless we regain our childhood, we miss the point of Christmas. Like children everywhere, they, too, wanted to go up into the attic. Here's what happened:

You're going up in the attic, Dad –
Please can I come too?
I'll even get the ladder, Dad,
And put it up for you.

Of all the places in our house
I love the attic best;
It's dark there – dark as Christmas
With every box a chest

Of surprise and promise –
The things we store up there
Are put away like memories
To open if you dare.

34

You're going up in the attic, Dad –
Can I come up too, *please!*
For hidden in the attic
Among the memories

Is part of me and part of you –
The part we seldom show;
Oh, up there in the attic, Dad,
Is all we're not, below.

May we never lose the wonder of going up into the attic. May we always be in touch with the child within.

That Empty Feeling

I'm not a Buddhist, but I believe that it's only in emptiness that all things are possible. A full vessel can hold no more. A person who is full of himself has exhausted his possibilities.

If I have a sense of emptiness, it has come from the village of my youth, Moyvane in Co. Kerry. When I was a child there in the 1950s, it was its emptiness that impressed me. An emptiness that I could fill with my imagination.

My parents had a small grocery opposite the creamery. The shop was busy in the mornings but, once the farmers had gone home, the shop was quiet as the village.

I was an only child; the village was my home. I'd wander around the village, coming and going as I pleased. There wasn't a kitchen in the village that I didn't know. The neighbours were kind – they'd give me tea and homemade bread. Indeed one, Kitty Shine, herself a shopkeeper, was kind enough to sprinkle a teaspoonful of white sugar on my bread and butter. Needless to say, to such an inveterate wanderer, the bread I got outside tasted better than the bread I got at home!

But my favourite place was Brosnan's Corner, right in the middle of the village. It was there we used gather to swap stories, to share our news and views, to pass around the surreptitious cigarette, though I must admit that I never became a smoker.

If my favourite place was Brosnan's Corner, my favourite time was Sunday afternoon. Long before Paul Simon wrote 'The Sound of Silence', I knew all about it. Picture me, a child at Brosnan's Corner on a lazy Sunday afternoon. The village is deserted. The pubs are closed. Many have gone to a local football match. Some have retired for a siesta. The faint sound of Micheál O'Hehir's voice from a village radio serves only to accentuate the silence. I am the companion of a stray dog and the occasional crow. Papers flutter in a crosswind at the corner. I am alone and I love it. In looking out at the village, I am looking in at myself. The village and I are one. All my life I've had this feeling. It informs all I do and think and say. The village of my childhood. The emptiness today.

A trap, a haycart and an empty street
(An image that I've carried all these years),
A greyhound at the corner where we'd meet –
A picture of the past, too deep for sneers.
Jimmy Nolan took that photo 'way back when
His camera was the only one around.
The village of my childhood. Once again
I'm a child, and this, my native ground,
Is empty as a Sunday afternoon
When pubs are closed and all are at the match;
I sit at Brosnan's Corner on my own
Empty as the street where I keep watch –
An emptiness he pictured like a poem;
An inward street: the street that leads to home.

Do Chum Ghlóire Dé agus Onóra na hÉireann

The last temptation is the greatest treason:
To do the right deed for the wrong reason.

Thus wrote T. S. Eliot in his play, *Murder in the Cathedral*, which was first published in 1935.

Community is the buzz word now. Everyone from politicians to priests uses it for their own ends. Mostly these ends are honourable. They are for the common good. But a community can be looked upon selfishly. There are votes in the community. Have you noticed how the roads get tarred before elections, how suddenly the picture brightens and there are promises of better times to come?

Karl Marx called religion 'the opium of the people'. Maybe he was right. People, particularly the disenfranchised, could be kept in line, used and abused by a clergy who manipulated their flock with promises of an eternal reward for temporal sacrifice. Now I'm all for sacrifice. Remember, we Catholics *assist* at the *sacrifice* of the mass. It is central to our world view. And we all know what it is to make sacrifices for our loved ones, deferring gratification or simply doing without for the love of others. But there is a difference between voluntary sacrifice and exploitation.

There is much talk nowadays about authority – or more

precisely, its lack. Reared in a hierarchical, patriarchal society, we fear for the future when its institutions crumble. But Christ, for instance, didn't found an institution. What he bequeathed to us was more a movable feast. He moved from place to place preaching, teaching, healing, blessing, bearing witness to the truth. I sometimes wonder whether our faith is not more in an institution than in the radical teachings of Christ.

Similarly with the law. We must, of course, respect the law at all times. But laws change. What was a crime yesterday is not a crime today and vice versa. In his poem 'Law Like Love', W. H. Auden compares law to love – we all need it, he says, but we seldom keep it! But then, Christ said that the just fall seven times a day and that we should forgive seventy times seven transgressions.

Which brings me back to community. There are very visible people out there who do great deeds, who dazzle with achievement. These are valuable people. They are necessary. But there are other, equally valuable, people who are invisible to the world at large. People who, day in, day out, persevere, doing good wherever they can, encouraging, inspiring, or just being plain there. John Milton (1608–1674) in his famous sonnet 'On His Blindness' (which isn't so much about his physical blindness, as his lack of poetic inspiration which he deemed necessary for him to serve God) asks 'Doth God exact day-labour, light denied?' But Patience replies:

> … God doth not need
> Either man's work or his own gifts. Who best
> Bear his mild yoke, they serve him best. His state
> Is kingly: thousands at his bidding speed,
> And post o'er land and ocean without rest;
> They also serve who only stand and wait.

In this mad world of rushing and fussing, it is good to remember that they also serve who only stand and wait.

Why should we serve our community? There are many reasons. We have mixed motives. We do it to give. And in giving, we receive. Maybe we do it for love – for love of what we're doing, for love of those we serve. In a world where the concept of love is debased almost beyond recognition, it is well to return to the words of Saint Paul. At a time when love had a specific meaning, before it was recruited into the service of sentimentality and even banality, we used the word 'charity' to describe a love for our neighbour, in the broad meaning of that word, and a willingness to aid those in need. By definition, it is personal and sympathetic. Saint Paul, in his first epistle to the Corinthians, writes:

> Though I speak with the tongues of men and of angels, and have not charity, I am become as sounding brass, or a tinkling cymbal.
>
> And though I have the gift of prophesy, and understand all mysteries, and all knowledge; and though I have all faith, so that I could remove mountains, and have not charity, I am nothing.
>
> And though I bestow all my goods to feed the poor, and though I give my body to be burned, and have not charity, it profiteth me nothing.

I suppose that those of us who are believers see the Christ in everybody and know that what we do to the least of His brethren, we do unto Him. So we involve ourselves in our communities *'do chum ghlóire Dé agus onóra na hÉireann'* as they used to say in the old days – 'for the glory of God and the honour of Ireland'. The right deed done for the right reason.

'No Man is an Island'

'No man is an island', the poet John Donne reminds us. We are all part of a community. The individual, to be truly fulfilled, must immerse himself or herself in the life of the community. For the community enriches us as we enrich it. Each of us expresses ourselves in our own way, and through us the community finds expression. A community, like a nation or 'the people of God', is an idea, and it cannot exist without its people – a people who work together, who play together, who pray together. I accept that not everyone in the community shares the same religious beliefs; I accept that we don't all worship in churches, but wasn't it the Romans who coined the phrase *laborare est orare* – 'to work is to pray'.

Consider, then, the people of a community going about their daily rounds. Creating their community. Re-creating themselves in their community. '*Ar scáth a chéile a mhaireann na daoine*', we say – 'people depend on each other'.

One very obvious expression of the community is its football team. I often get the feeling that when a parish or a county team takes the field, for one hour it becomes the expression, the incarnation of its parish or county. The boys and girls, the men and women who make up these teams lose, as it were, their individual identity as they become a team – the visible expression of their community. And that is why we get so passionate about the game: because it is ourselves we see out there on the field. Our team wearing our colours are not just individuals: they are, in a mystical way, the physical expression of their community. This means the players and spectators are really one, that it's the community as an *idea* – the community's idea of itself, that takes the field. And when we win, the cup is not merely a trophy to be lost or won in the course of a game of football – it becomes a kind of grail, in the religious sense: in a very real sense, that cup is holy – something we have striven for, something we have hoped for, something which we may even have prayed for, something for which we have given our very best; and that cup symbolises all that's good and beautiful in the game – the highest honour the game can bestow. Because when a cup comes to a county or parish, it flows with the heart's desire: the community celebrates – songs are made and sung, the deeds of the past are recalled, we rejoice in the present, and we face the future with joyful hope. And all because a group of individuals came together as a team.

This happens in every parish, in every county. And I'm not just talking about football or sports. Communities manifest themselves in a multiplicity of ways – each community according to its genius. They may do so in the arts – in drama groups, in music making, in dancing, in singing, in storytelling; they may do so in the pride they take in their environment – caring for their streets and streams, their houses, hills and hedges; they manifest it in the way they care for each other. In this, of course, they follow Christ for inasmuch as we do to one of the least of his brethren, we do unto him.

A community must have an idea of itself. It must know who it is and where it is going. Therefore all the members of the community have an invaluable contribution to make. The mystical body of the community is made up of all its members. Thus the community finds its own way, its own truth, its own life.

And in every community you will find leaders – people who selflessly devote themselves to the good of their people. Cynics might wonder what's in it for those leaders; 'they must be getting something out of it' they whisper. And the answer to that is yes! they are. To do good is its own reward. To see your community working together, saying itself, playing itself, praying itself, is beautiful. And beauty, as John Keats has written, is a joy forever.

13

Up Down!

Moyvane, Co. Kerry. September 1959. I was six years old and Kerry had just won the All Ireland Senior Football Final. We were the greatest as we shouted 'Up Kerry!' the length and breadth of the village. The Kerry team weren't mortal – they were gods and they walked among us every day. We lived in our own story – the story of football which had its own mysteries and today they were glorious. We had resurrected from defeat and ascended into heaven where we were crowned champions of all Ireland. We would live in that reflected glory all year.

It was 1960 and I had just turned seven. At seven you think that all things can be known. Growing in facts if not in knowledge, I regarded the world as a sure and certain place, a place of predictable outcomes, a world of black and white. In this world, Moyvane was the centre and Kerry were the greatest. It was 1960 and I'd never even heard of County Down.

Things were changing in the village in 1960. By then the village had 'the electric light'; our Yanks began to visit us from New York and New Orleans; and a new water scheme was begun. It was proposed to pump water from the river Gale below the village to a huge water tower which was being built in Collins' field up the Glin Road which would supply the whole parish. Among the many things we learned that summer were new names. Now a caterpillar was no longer just a creepy-crawly that ate cabbage, it was a great big track machine; surnames we'd never heard of in our parish now came to work among us

– names like Seán Treacy and especially Malachy McMullen.

Malachy McMullen drove the Caterpillar. He spoke in a funny accent. We were fascinated by it. We imitated his accent and we teased him because of it. He took it in great part. To us, he was simply not a Kerryman. Later we would know he hailed from County Down.

One Monday morning that summer, Malachy McMullen had a red and black flag flying on his Caterpillar. We children wondered what it was. It was the Down colours. They were playing Kerry in the All Ireland Football Final.

Down? Where in the name of God was that? What sort of a name for a county was Down? How would you shout for them? 'Up Down?' Is that what you'd cheer? 'Up Down! Up Down!' we teased Malachy McMullen as we passed.

There were no televisions in Moyvane in 1960. Only radios. The streets were abandoned to the stray dogs as the whole village tuned into Radio Éireann for the match broadcast. Such names on the Down team as we'd never heard before – Eamonn McKay, Kevin Mussen, Tony Hadden were all strange music to our southern ears. The strange music won that day. Our gods were overthrown.

Even now I can remember facing Malachy McMullen the following morning. It wasn't so much that Down had won, as that Kerry were beaten. Beaten! We had no answer to the strange music. The following year, that music won again.

By then we knew that the world was not sure and certain, that things weren't black and white. It was a valuable lesson, one of the many we learned from football. There would be more lessons to learn but I'll never forget the summer when our gods were overthrown – the first step taken on the way of the unknown.

14

Tread Softly on my Dreams

All Ireland Final Sunday, 1962. A very different Ireland to today. An Ireland without computers, playstations or private cars. An Ireland that was waking up to the wonder of television.

There was no television in Moyvane in September 1962. Most people had no car. The creamery manager, Paddy Sugrue, our next-door neighbour, had. We were all football mad. We'd tune in to Radio Éireann and live the football match, catch by catch, kick by kick, score by score to the voice of Mícheál O'Hehir. We'd do it again today as Kerry togged out against Roscommon in Croke Park.

Croke Park! The very sound of it was magic to our ears. Croke Park was a kind of heaven where men became colossi, and mortals became gods in the mystery of Gaelic football. Even today, at a remove of over forty years, I can line out that Kerry team: Johnny Culloty, Seamus Murphy, Niall Sheehy, Tim 'Tiger' Lyons, Seán Óg Sheehy, Noel Lucey, Mick O'Dwyer, Mick O'Connell, Jimmy Lucey, Dan McAuliffe, Timmie O'Sullivan, Gerry O'Riordan, Garry McMahon, Tom Long, Paudie Sheehy. That team photograph, published with the players' autographs *as Gaeilge* in the *Irish Independent* after the All Ireland and sold as a souvenir subsequently, hangs on the wall of my study. I bought it in Margaret Walsh's newsagents in Moyvane shortly after the All Ireland and kept it at home until I married and moved out. My father had it mounted and hung it up in his utility room. He gave it to my son John a few years before he died and I asked John to give it to me last year.

The reason I wanted it for myself again was that I was writing a sonnet about football, what it meant to us at that time, and what it still means to some of us today. The team of 1962 weren't in it for the money. 'One for the money, two for the show' goes Carl Perkins' song. Well, whatever about the show, those men weren't playing football for money. They loved the game, as we did; they believed in the game, as we did. Beaten finalists in 1960 and again beaten – and again by Down – in the semi-final in 1961, a victorious Joe Lennon proclaimed that Kerry football was years out of date. Well, it wasn't! Nor is it today.

In the sonnet, I tried to convey something of that day in September 1962. As I said, most people in the village had no motor car. There was no television in the village. Paddy Sugrue found out that an enterprising curate in Shanagolden in west Limerick had a television set installed in the local parish hall and that you could pay to see the game there. (This was a time between the sale of indulgences and the advent of bingo, and the poor man had hit on a sure-fire way of making a few bob for his parish). Paddy Sugrue loaded his family and myself into his car and drove us to Shanagolden. The hall was packed – west Limerick people are as football-passionate as any Kerry folk. We gazed as the wonder of television grew in our hearts and minds. The ball was thrown in, the game was on. Garry McMahon scored the fastest goal ever scored in an All Ireland Football Final. When the final whistle blew, Kerry had won the game by one goal and twelve points to one goal and six. The game, the historians tell us, wasn't up to much. A contemporary account (John D. Hickey's) describes it as 'as long as a month of wet Sundays; the most undistinguished, cheerless, unexciting and insipid All Ireland Final ever played'. But to a child watching his first All Ireland Final, and watching the newly introduced television at the same time, this was the stuff of dreams. And it's dreams, not facts, that sustain us. To this day, I can recall that hall, that crowd, that television, that match, that victory. I know there will be small boys and girls (I was nine years old in September 1962) who will be watching such finals in the years to come. I hope they will be worthy of their dreams.

THE TEAM OF 'SIXTY-TWO
for Garry McMahon

No logo here on jersey, togs or boot,
A team who played for pure love of a game
That reveals its players in their truth,
A team that asked no money, handled fame.
We got a lift to the wonder of TV,
To a distant village, a small set in the hall,
We paid like all the others just to see
Our team's ascent to glory raise us all.
For we believed in heroes 'way back then
Who raised themselves to immortality;
Before me in that photo, fifteen men
Who from my youth were more than men to me.
That picture hangs where once a saint or pope
Would look down from the wall in pious hope.

Up for the Match: The All-Ireland Senior Football Final 1984

It was all over at 5 p.m. When Ambrose O'Donovan received the Sam Maguire cup on behalf of Kerry, the point was made: the game was clean, the hill was quiet, order prevailed. Even if the game was more dogged than inspired, it was, so far, a quiet day.

Jack O'Shea headed for the Outside Broadcasting Unit amid much jostling and hugging and kissing. The supporters evacuated Croke Park. It was 5.10 p.m.

A silent evacuation by All Ireland standards, the Kerry supporters mostly smiling and remarking to one another: 'This was sweet', and undefeated Dublin supporters all streaming down towards North Frederick Street and Parnell Square.

It was 5.20 p.m. and the Kerry supporters had, as always, congregated outside the Belvedere and Barry's hotels. Johnny Walsh of Ballylongford, a stalwart of many a Kerry victory in the 1940s, stood with his son Barry, himself a former Kerry player, and a group of friends on the footpath outside the Belvedere. I stood there, too, waiting for a friend.

Streams of blue festooned Dublin supporters strode by, rightly proud of their team and county. There was occasional good humoured banter between the Kerrymen and the Dubs: 'It's a long way back to Kerry,' they joked; and we: 'It's a longer way back for the Dubs.'

It was 5.30 p.m. and a battalion of young Dublin supporters sang their way down the street. By now the Belvedere was crowded with Kerry supporters, and the steps leading to the front door were crowded with Kerry men, women and youths, many of whom were waiting to rendezvous with more tardy companions. The singing battalion approached the Belvedere. One of the leading standard bearers spat at the Kerry supporters on the path. No one took much notice: this was just an isolated obscenity to be taken in the spirit of the day. Johnny Walsh and his group remained in conversation.

The singing stopped. The Dubs, armed with flags, faced the Kerry supporters. Silence. Silence. Then loudly: 'Ye filth, ye filth', chanted the Dublin mob.

'If we were Glasgow Rangers supporters, this would be war', quipped someone on the steps a little nervously. 'Ye filth, ye filth', the chant continued. The Kerry group held ranks.

No more banter: this was confrontation – 'Ye filth, ye filth', from the Dubs; 'Go home and take yere *batin'*', from the Kerry crowd.

One blue clad supporter flew through the air and planted a drop kick, Kung Fu style, on one of the Kerry lads. When he landed, the two wrestled briefly. Bruce Lee was repelled. There was no retaliation.

'Ye filth, ye filth', howled the fifty-strong blue contingent. The people on the steps began to withdraw into the Belvedere Hotel. In a matter of minutes all the Kerry supporters would have been inside. There would be no broken limbs or broken windows today. I was in the front row. The blue ranks broke. Blue flags became cudgels and rained upon our heads. We protected ourselves. We repulsed the attack. We did not retaliate.

The blues reformed. 'Come on, come on', they taunted us with Gary Glitter's song. We didn't. It was not cowardice. The

Belvedere was full of Kerrymen and, when it comes to brawling, Kerrymen can give as good as they get. 'Come on, come on', the taunt continued. We didn't. There were half a dozen or so of us left on the steps. The man beside me was wearing the Kerry colours – a green and gold cap. The only emblem that any of us left on the steps was wearing. 'Come on, come on.' We shook our heads. There were no more blows.

By now, the management of the Belvedere Hotel was aware of what was happening. A porter came to the door and requested that the man with the green and gold cap either remove it or leave the steps. He ordered us all indoors. We stood on the steps facing Barry's Hotel.

Inexplicably, the blue battalion moved on. There was a sound of breaking glass as they smashed the windows of a parked car. A few gardaí arrived – too few, too late. It was 5.36 p.m.

16

Winning isn't Everything

I have often wondered why people play football, write poetry, sing songs, dance or make music. They begin, possibly, in imitation of the great – some admired footballer, poet, singer, dancer or musician. Some fall by the wayside early through lack of dedication or talent. Some persevere. Why? At this stage it's gone beyond the imitation of the great. It's an expression of the self. Human nature being what it is, the footballer, poet or whoever, desires the greatest theatre in which to express his art. For the Gaelic footballer, this must be Croke Park on All Ireland Final day. Most of the greatest players have graced that stage. They are hailed as heroes, garlanded as champions, commemorated in song and story. They have had their reward.

But there are others – footballers, poets, singers, dancers, musicians – who are different. Artists whose belief in, and com-mitment to, themselves and their community, their club, their county, is so strong that they are not tempted by the lure of accolade. Artists who stick with their own; people who don't need medals or trophies in order to believe in themselves or their community.

At the Munster Football Semi-Final between Kerry and Limerick played in the Gaelic grounds, Limerick, on 12 June 2002, this came home very powerfully to me. Our highly regarded midfield was getting a fair old game of it from the Limerick pair of John Quane and John Galvin. I was impressed by John Quane in particular. On the way out of the stadium,

I was talking to my old friend and singing *compadre,* Johnny Mullane, of Athea, who played at centre forward on that great Limerick team which nearly stole a march on Kerry in the Munster Football Final of 1965. I asked him about John Quane. He told me that he played for Galtee Gaels, a stone's throw from the Cork border; and that, had he chosen to, he could have played for Cork, thereby increasing his chances of All Ireland success a hundred fold. But he didn't. He chose to play for his native Limerick. As a Moyvane man, equally committed to my local community, I feel I know why he chose Limerick over Cork. I have tried to express it in the following poem:

A FOOTBALLER

He could have played with better
But he chose his own;
Playing with his county
He'd never carry home

The trophy all aspire to
But that's not why he played:
If he played with another county
He'd feel he had betrayed

Himself, his art, his people,
So he plays out his career
Away from the glare of headlines.
And yet sometimes you'll hear

From followers of football
The mention of his name.
It's enough that they believe in him,
His way, his truth, his game.

Winning isn't everything! Ask John Quane.

17

Schooldays

On my first day at school, I ran away. Or perhaps I should say I never even got into the school. Even now, at a distance of more than forty years, I can remember that first day. Being a child of above normal curiosity, I was, naturally, looking forward to my first day in school. I had been told all sorts of quaint and curious stories about school. I had learned, too, that only 'babies' stayed at home. One's first day in school was the first giant step into the wide and wonderful world of adulthood. And so, December 1957 came; I turned five and was surrendered by my parents to that wide and wonderful world.

In those days, infants were not usually accompanied to school by fond and fretful mums on that awesome day. I was entrusted to the care of seasoned and sturdy schoolboys who policed me down Main Street, around Nunan's Corner and up Glin Road, up the frosty hill and in the school gate.

As my escort comprised children of higher classes, and as none of them was bound for the infant room, they began giving me detailed instructions as to how to negotiate my way through the school to the infant room. Being then, as now, totally useless at following instructions, I quickly became confused. Confusion grew to irritation which, inevitably, turned to panic. And up ahead loomed, large as dread, the big, green door. I bolted.

Of course, I had the advantage of surprise, and was at the school gate before my escort knew what was happening. I was also, happily, unencumbered by bag or baggage or any appurtenance likely to hinder a youngster sprinting for freedom, and I rounded Nunan's Corner before any of my pursuers.

But the problem then was, how was I to go home and face Mam and Dad? I was pretty sure I'd get a sympathetic hearing from Dad, but Mam was a terror for education – what words of mine could mollify her? (Even then I knew that it wasn't so much a question of what you did, as the words you could muster in your defence that really mattered).

Anyway, to make a long story short, I sneaked in home and faced the music. Naturally, I can't remember what formula of words I used, but they must have been pretty convincing for I wasn't frog-marched back to school that day, or the next day, or the day after.

In fact, I didn't take my seat in low infants until after April 1958 and, after an initial bad reaction, I settled into the swing of things pretty easily.

*

On 1 July 1975, I walked down Main Street, turned Nunan's Corner, walked up Glin Road, up the hill and entered through the green door to begin another term in school – this time on the other side of the desk. I was twenty-two and brimful of that blend of fire and naiveté that springs eternal in a young man's breast. Now I have always held that without a dollop of naiveté nothing gets done. There comes a time when the only way forward is through faith and hope – sometimes in the face of overwhelming odds. Faith and hope despite overwhelming odds imply a certain naiveté – that native optimism, that native belief that things will turn out well. And so I set out, if not to change the world, at least to change Moyvane. As was thought proper for a teacher, particularly a young male teacher at that time, I joined the local GAA club where I quickly became trainer of juvenile football teams and a selector of the senior football team; I put on concerts, joined the local development association, and so on. What changed? The under-16 team got into the north Kerry Final (which they lost); the seniors won the north Kerry League; the development association flourished for a while and then folded (it has since been revived). In other words, nothing changed. Or so it appeared.

But the real contribution a teacher, or anyone for that matter, can make is in the minds and hearts of those they touch. If some of my naiveté has touched my pupils, I won't have wasted my time; if some of my optimism has touched my pupils, I won't have wasted my time; if some of my curiosity has touched my pupils, I won't have wasted my time.

And what have I got in return? I have been touched by my pupils: by their sense of trust, by their honesty, by their atrocious unpredictability, their verve, their zest, their exuberance, by their sheer love of life. Now I believe that a teacher cannot be a teacher unless he is capable of learning from, and with, his pupils.

For all I have learned from, and with, my pupils, I am truly grateful. It has been worthwhile.

18

Inner Pain

Have you ever wondered how much of what we adults try to impart to children really sinks in? We try to civilise them, to educate their moral and aesthetic sense, to develop their social skills and so on. As a teacher I sometimes think that the children learn in spite of us.

How often has a parent or teacher advised a child only to be ignored? How often have we admonished them only to be disobeyed? It seems to me that the human being, young or old, has an inherent dislike of being told what to do – and often that's what we adults do to children, whether we realise it or not. Of course much of this is necessary: children must be guided, persuaded, influenced, taught. But we shouldn't be surprised when the child consciously (by disobeying us) or unconsciously (by heedlessness) calls 'enough'.

One of the areas where we adults, particularly teachers, are called upon to influence children is in the field of religion. While we acknowledge that the primary educators are the parents in the home, very often it is left to teachers to cultivate the religious sensibilities of the child.

In our primary schools, religion is taught every day. I am reminded of the story told by a former parish priest who, on a visit to a Catholic school in England, visited the infants' class. He spoke to them about Jesus. Suddenly a child interjected. 'Please sir,' he said to the priest, 'what channel is he on?' We haven't quite slipped to that stage in Ireland, but we may be getting there.

An incident from our own school comes to mind. The curate, a young, sincere, pious man, was endeavouring to convey the subtleties of the paschal mystery to a group of six year olds some years ago. He visited their classroom during Holy Week. 'What week is this?' he beamed. The children hadn't a clue. 'What Sunday is next Sunday?' he persevered. 'Easter Sunday, Father,' was the eager reply. 'What's special about Easter Sunday?' the priest continued. In one voice they shouted 'Easter eggs, Father!' Unperturbed, the curate continued. He brought them back to Good Friday. 'What happened on Good Friday?' he enquired. All the children knew. They spouted out a grizzly tale of blood and guts, and spears and whips and crowns of thorns. 'Yes children,' the curate replied. 'That's outer pain – like when you fall in the yard, or when you cut yourself. But Jesus suffered inner pain too – he was sad, he was rejected, he felt alone. All those things are inner pain. Did any boy or girl here ever suffer inner pain?' Slowly from the middle of the class, a lone hand was raised. Almost in a whisper a little girl spoke: 'Yes Father – when you get constipation!' The voice of experience. A lesson learned.

19

Creating the Conscience of the Race: a Portrait of the Artist as a National School Teacher

The idea of religion is just not important any more. Well-off people now want a well-rounded education for their children … It suits modern, working parents that a school provides everything under one roof, and they just have to write a cheque to cover it.

– The Irish Times, 7 March 1998

I doubt that many of my colleagues, who are national, for which read primary, school teachers, are 'into' Joyce, or for that matter, into modernism. It isn't just that we are living in a post-modernist age; it is more a matter, I suspect, of Joyce being a difficult writer. Teachers, I believe, read as much to unwind after a demanding day in school as to educate themselves in the modernist, or any other, canon.

Joyce was identified by Dillon Johnston in his book, *Irish Poetry After Joyce,* as the father of contemporary Irish poetry. There's a case to be made for that (though I think that Theo Dorgan's *Irish Poetry Since Kavanagh* strikes a necessary balance, as Kavanagh's influence on modern Irish poetry has been significant). However, there *is* a case to be made that Joyce has had a significant influence on Irish poetry. For two reasons: Joyce, in his celebration of the ordinary, has set the tone for much of what is best in contemporary Irish poetry; secondly, and of more import, is his notion of the epiphany – the sudden elevation of the ordinary to the extra-ordinary, of the revelation of the work of art, of art as the essential vision.

Joyce was a Catholic, educated by Jesuits, wounded by his education. He eventually chose exile from his country, from his religion. He had to in order to 'forge in the smithy of [his] soul the uncreated conscience of [his] race'. That word 'forge' has always interested me. Its other meaning of 'to fake' is never far away. Which leads to the question of what art is. The history of art is not without its instances of forgeries and hoaxes being accepted as the real thing. Indeed, there is a sense that art is part forgery. In literature we sometimes call the end product (the 'text' if you like) a 'fiction' – which itself has connotations of faking. Would it be to push things too far to suggest that when the critic Declan Kiberd talks about 'Inventing Ireland', that there is a necessary fiction? that the way we perceive ourselves and our society is itself a fiction? and that this fiction making is not necessarily bad? We live by a set of images that we partly receive, and partly create for ourselves. We forge (in both senses) these images in the smithies of our souls. Inventing Ireland may be no more than creating an agreed fiction by which we can live with ourselves and, ultimately, with each other. Anyway, Joyce had to go into exile to create the conscience of his race.

But, in a sense, we all are exiles. Joyce, a Catholic, would have known this – after all, Catholics pray in the 'Hail Holy Queen' about life as 'our exile'. Joyce chose a physical as well as an existential one. The teachers teaching in our national, or primary, schools today have stayed put. They haven't upped and gone. I know that times have changed. I know that Joyce suffered at the hands of Irish society – from censorship laws, from cowardly printers and publishers – but the fact is he left.

The teachers now teaching in our schools (and they number many creative artists, including writers, among them) have chosen to stay. Indeed, John McGahern, forced to resign as a national teacher, opted eventually to live in Ireland and to write from here. It is a sign of a better Ireland, an Ireland where free speech is taken for granted, where writers and other artists needn't live in fear of censorship, an Ireland that supports its creative artists. The climate has changed for the better.

The title of this chapter is taken from *A Portrait of the Artist as a Young Man*. What I want to suggest is that the teacher is an artist, too. Many years ago, it was suggested to me by a former teacher of mine (who was anxious that teaching wouldn't destroy what he perceived as a talent I had for writing – a man who is himself a prominent artist) that he was disappointed in his fellow teachers on the grounds that they wasted their gifts in walking greyhounds and running football teams. He was concerned for their untapped potential, their undeveloped (or, at least, under-developed) talents. I want to examine this. The primary definition of art in the *Concise Oxford Dictionary* is 'a human creative skill or its application'; and an artist is defined as one who 'practises any of the arts'. By this definition, teaching is an art and teachers are artists. By this definition even walking greyhounds and running football teams can be an art. Let me explain. We are coming to see art nowadays not just as an individual expression of the self, but also as a community activity. The teacher is often the one who facilitates this activity. To borrow a phrase from the Roman Catholic mass, it is 'through him, with him, in him' that this activity happens. Thus the teacher walking greyhounds or running football teams may be the catalyst for the appreciation of the poetry of greyhound racing or football, and is very likely an influential member of the 'doggy' fraternity or the football fraternity. Fairly mundane work, but it facilitates the work of art.

Because football is art. Greyhounds ('the poor man's racehorses'!) too. Here are two poems that deal with football as art – one as individual epiphany, the other as an epiphany of the community.

In the first poem, 'Dancing Through', I suggest that the footballer, in this case Kerry's Mikey Sheehy, is an artist creating his own space, a space in which to express himself as he solos to the goal (in every sense of that word):

DANCING THROUGH
Homage to Mikey Sheehy, Footballer

Nureyev with a football,
You solo to the goal
Where the swell of expectation
Spurts in vain –
O master of the ritual,
O flesh of tribal soul,
Let beauty be at last
Released from pain ...

Now grace eludes its marker
Creating its own space
While grim defenders
Flounder in its wake;
And the ball you won from conflict
Yields to your embrace –
Goal beckons like a promise ...
And you take.

In the second poem, 'At the Ball Game' (a title, incidentally, that I took from another modernist, William Carlos Williams), I look at the communal epiphany which sometimes happens at football matches. John B. Keane many years ago suggested that

I write a poem about a north Kerry Football final. I declined, saying that I would need to write about it as a search for the Holy Grail. John B. dismissed such a notion and initiated ('blooded' is the word we use for it in Kerry) me into the secret of football. It would have to be an epic, he said, an *Iliad* about the battle between two parishes. But, I discovered, there's more to it than that. There's more to football than doing battle and winning. Winning is only the beginning. It's how you win that counts; it's what is revealed in the process that counts. It's football, not as sport but as art.

AT THE BALL GAME

Everything out there you see
Is a version of reality
As heroes triumph over doubt
And bring their kind of truth about.

Each, according to his way,
Engages on the field of play,
And, urging on, the faithful crowd
Are cheering, praising, cursing loud
For beauty only will suffice,
Beauty to infuse our lives:
No cup, no trophy will redeem
Victory by ignoble means.

And, so, we take the field today
To find ourselves in how we play,
Out there on the field to be
Ourselves, a team, where all can see;
For nothing is but is revealed
And tested on the football field.

The art of the teacher here is to apply his skills creatively, to inspire his community both as a group and as individuals to achieve its goal – the goal of self expression, the goal of living creatively, of living beautifully in your own place. This isn't just about football or greyhounds, it's about re-creating yourself in your own environment, and thus creating (or inventing) your own community. I apologise here for the maleness of my vocabulary. Women teachers have achieved everything that men have in this regard. Indeed, their influence is all the greater, as they outnumber men in the teaching profession. My only defence is that I speak for myself, and thus, unavoidably, as a man.

Community involvement is but one aspect of the teacher's art. What about the teacher in the classroom? Creating the conscience of the race? Indeed. More and more, as the work of not just educating, but rearing children is off-loaded on to teachers, this is precisely what we are doing. In national schools, we teach religion, relationships and sex education, the Stay Safe programme which helps children to identify and report abuse, physical education and all the creative and academic subjects prescribed by the *Curriculum for Primary Schools*. For better or worse, we are a huge influence on children's lives (how often has a harassed parent been silenced by the simple statement 'But teacher said it'?). There isn't full agreement on what the primary school curriculum should contain. Should national schools (effectively state schools) teach denominational religion? Should we teach relationships and sex education, thus, it is alleged, taking away from the role of parents as the primary educators of their children? Because, in doing so, we are, incontrovertibly, creating the conscience of the race.

I don't want to get bogged down in the above arguments (they have been well rehearsed in public for a long time); but if we are to create a pluralist society, a society that can live with itself and with others, these questions are vital. If we are to re-invent Ireland, we will have to learn to live with ourselves and with others. We don't exist in a vacuum – we all come from somewhere. My own feeling, and that of many teachers, both Protestant and Catholic, is that we must first have a sense of ourselves and our own traditions before we can embrace the other. Nothing will come of nothing. If we are to create a new set of images by which we can agree to imagine ourselves, it behoves us to have an authentic self image first.

We are constantly defining, and re-defining, ourselves in our relationships with ourselves and with others. Teachers (good ones anyway) help children to define themselves in relation to themselves, their families, their friends, their community and their environment. Beginning with the self, a good teacher will build the pupil's self esteem and confidence, thus enabling the child to 'inform its conscience' (a phrase much used by the Catholic Church), or in more secular terms, to make informed choices. The 1971 *Curriculum for Primary Schools* exhorted teachers to instil a national pride in their pupils. (Patriotism was an OK word back then!) Nowadays we speak less of patriotism, afraid of much of the baggage that word has accumulated in the twentieth century. Facing into a new *New Curriculum for Primary Schools*, we will have to reclaim words like patriotism. As religion declines, as belief in God declines, the importance of the teacher as a sower of values increases. In an increasingly secular world, the teacher may be the only one who stimulates and fosters the children's innate spirituality. In Ireland, we still do this through the teaching of religion in most schools. But we also do it through the arts; indeed, the teaching of religion in most Catholic schools is inextricably linked with the arts, particularly poetry, painting, drawing, mime, song, dance and storytelling. If mere anarchy is not to be loosed upon the world, the teacher's role as a spiritual father, or mother, must be recognised and supported.

It is not enough for education to reflect society – it must lead it. The politics of education must become the education of politics, all the more so with educational policy pointing to greater participation across the board – from politicians, priests, parents and pedagogues. We must ensure a fully round-ed, liberal education for our children. Indeed, a famous green paper on education raised the fear in many teachers that school was to become some kind of factory to be judged using industrial criteria. Teachers will have to stand up for teaching as an art, and not merely some utilitarian process whereby units are discharged into the workforce.

I have said that education must lead, not so much reflect, society. This, by definition, is what education is. This demands much of teachers as artists. Creatively, it demands that teachers constantly educate themselves, that they find within themselves the resources, the art, to lead society. National teachers have been prominent in all aspects, artistic and otherwise, of Irish life. Their greatest loneliness is their greatest strength. Enclosed all day in their classrooms, these classrooms become, in Seamus Heaney's phrase, republics of conscience where teachers and pupils engage in a democratic (if guided by the teacher) explora-tion of themselves in their environment.

It is now hoped to replace the 1971 curriculum in the light of current views of the philosophy and methodology of education. Again, teachers will implement the curriculum, again we will bear the brunt of whatever criticism is levelled, again we will experience the lonely satisfaction of seeing a job well done. This *New Curriculum* will be created in partnership. The NCCA (National Council for Curriculum and Assessment) committees who are devising this new curriculum consist of teachers, parents, representatives of the Department of Education, the churches and other interested partners in education; in this way, the teacher has a real voice in this curriculum.

The conscience of the race is not a fixed entity. It is subject to change. As we become more educated, our perceptions change. Teachers will have to be ever more aware of the burden of educating the children of the new Ireland. In an ever more secular and selfish world, we will have to live the virtues and values of community life; in an ever more hectic world, we will have to live the values of patience and perseverance. This is our vocation – not, I hasten to add, to bore people out of their minds, but to open up the possibility of the full (or, at least, the fuller) life.

Catholics (Joyce would have known this) speak of the informed conscience; in his time, that implied submitting to the Church of Rome. Nowadays, an informed conscience means having the wherewithal to make informed choices. This, today, is what conscience means. The teacher as educator, as model, as inspiration, plays an ever more vital role in creating this conscience. There may be no Joyces among our national teachers – in any case, after Joyce there can never be another. But there are artists among us – poets, playwrights, novelists, painters, musicians, singers, dancers, people who use their creative skills. The greatest teachers aren't afraid to let their pupils climb on their shoulders. Because to teach is to hope. To teach is to have faith. To teach is to love. We set out to change the world. At least, we influence others, we give them a right of way into a vision of a greater world where the harmonies of art obtain. In creating the conscience of the race, we invent ourselves, artificers to a man – and woman! Teaching, like all art, changes nothing and it changes everything. That is the loneliness of the teacher, that is the loneliness of the artist. We do it because we must, because it is good. It is its own reward.

(Written in 2000)

20

The Poet in the Classroom

It was suggested to me as a bright, not altogether motivated leaving cert. student, by my mother who was very bright and very motivated, that the best thing somebody like myself could do would be to go into teaching, whereby I would go into a training college, as they were called at the time, and be supervised. She was rather worried that if I had the freedom of a university I would go off the rails as many a person did before, and so I went into teaching with my two eyes closed and didn't get them opened for a long time. It was some time before I discovered that teaching is actually a joy and that teaching is not a profession. We like to call ourselves in union terms, trade union terms, professionals, and we deserve to be treated as professionals in trade union terms, but there's a larger dimension to life than trade unionism. Teaching is an art, because a profession is something you do for money, and it finishes at a certain time, and teaching isn't like that; teaching is a full time vocation, it's something that you live with, something, possibly, that you die with – I'm not far enough along the road with that yet to know, but I do know that virtually anything significant that I've learned in my life has been learned through teaching.

*

I came out of the education system as a dedicated, bright, lazy leaving certer with five honours, and I knew nothing. I wasn't educated. I didn't know the weeds that were under my feet. I didn't know the stars that were over my head. When I came to teaching, because of the enlightenment of the 1971 curriculum, I found that I had to teach these things; so suddenly, I knew what Orion was, I knew what Sirius was, I knew what Cassiopeia was, I knew what the various weeds under my feet were and I knew the flowers. It seems to me that that's a far greater challenge to somebody: to incorporate the flowers of your life and the stars of your life into your being rather than the facts that we were taught. It seems to me that we were taught very much like a quiz team would be (it's a metaphor I often use): that you read so many books of so many facts and you spit them out rather like you'd press a button on a word processor or a computer and it spits out the information, but you actually know nothing about that information. It seemed to me to be an altogether more wholesome way of teaching that we would begin with the groundsel and the dock leaves and herb Robert, and go from there to the stars and, suddenly, it's under your feet and over your head, and it struck me as being a joyful way to live and a very challenging way to live, and I'm delighted now to be a teacher although I had no notion of what I was getting into when I first began teaching.

*

I have always believed in something that I used to call anarchy, but actually that's not the right word for it. 'Anarchy' I suggest, need not imply 'chaos' – I would see a difference between chaos, which is unruly mayhem, and anarchy. However, from the Greek, anarchy means 'without a leader', and that's where my argument falls down because I am the leader. Should I then say that what I believe in is a creative allowing people to be: that's what I try to do with the children in the class – I try to allow them to be themselves. I try to allow them to express themselves, to say themselves, to sing themselves, to draw themselves, to kick the football their own way, to do handstands their own way. I try to do that, but the question then is, how do you prevent that from becoming a total free-for-all, a total chaos? I must remain their friend, I must maintain their confidence, I must remain their confidant, I must remain somebody to whom they can feel free to say 'I don't like school', 'I don't like you'.

*

I must remain somebody that remains educable, because the danger with teaching is that the teacher becomes Sir Oracle. As Shakespeare said, 'I am Sir Oracle, and when I ope my lips let no dog bark' – the danger is that we become that; that is the real challenge to teaching, and the real stress – the stress is good, the stress is to allow these people to educate you. The danger is that we see children as little things that are to be programmed, and they're not: these are people who have their own perceptions, these are people who have their own feelings, these are people who have their own reactions, and they react to me, and they feel to me in their own way, and I am required by my own conscience to take that on board. The moral dilemma is how much right have I to impose myself on them – I have a duty to teach them good manners, I have a duty to teach them certain facts that they need to know, I have a duty to lead them out, as education leads them out, of themselves to a greater possibility because the child's world is, of itself, a narrow and subjective and often selfish world. I have a duty to do all these things – and that's what the stress is, but it's also a challenge: do you see what I mean by stress now? – it's not the old thing of people coming at you, managers at you and parents at you, that doesn't bother me; they don't come at me. I'm allowed to lead these children out of themselves to the best of my ability, and I'm deeply grateful for that.

*

I tell the story sometimes of how greatly I have been educated by young people. I was inside in my class one day many years ago, at the beginning of my career as a teacher, the opening of

70

my eyes as a teacher, and I was flogging an Irish poem to death. There were some children in the class who were as close to getting that poem as they ever would be, but I wanted more. So here was Sir Oracle imposing his will and his anger on these four children, and one of them, a girl, stood up and said to me, you know, she just stood up and she said: 'The trouble with you is you think you're the biggest man in the whole world.' And she was right; you know, the danger, the real occupational hazard of teaching is that we make ourselves into the biggest people in the whole world, and of course we're not. I had a huge crisis of professionalism and art and vocation and conscience, and I saw, yeah, that child was right. I dare not impose my standards on people who can't achieve them. There are people in my class who can achieve greater than I will; there are people in my class who can do as well as I can, and did; there are people who never will – this is in the academic sense, because the unfortunate thing about school is that it is still academically orientated. My way of getting around the tyranny of the academic is to enable people to open up artistically and, you know, the situation was that I was imposing an academic tyranny on people who weren't academic at all.

*

I have come up with a philosophy of life. I was talking to you earlier about living the Christian story: the Christian story is a great metaphor for life. In the 'Hail Holy Queen', we say 'mourning and weeping in this valley of tears' and if you look at life objectively, it seems to me that all the great writers and all the great musicians and all the great artists (and all the great religious) have come from difficulty to enlightenment: that seems to me to be the story of a significant life. Many people talk of happiness as being the goal of life, or some people do, and it seems to me that happiness is a very shallow concept because happiness is only happy: joy comes from deeper. Happiness comes from its own elevated nothingness. That's an awful thing to say, but I think maybe if I can say what joy means you might understand what I'm saying.

Joy comes from a real sense of what life is about; joy comes from a sense of the real and utter existential pain of living – separation, perhaps, from a god, an ideal, love, or authentic existence. We're all faced with this, and we all have to transcend it, and that's what joy is. And I had that in my own life. I mean, for various reasons, going through life I've felt rejected, I've felt depressed, I've felt outcast; it didn't appear much from the outside because I have a reasonably good control of my appearance, but from the inside it felt like outcast, it felt like depression, it felt like all the rest. How do you re-create your life? The Christian story tells us that Christ died; it goes from a God to a death to a resurrection, and I believe in God. So there was a death in my life – the death of my own personal beliefs – not just religious beliefs, but my own belief in myself. The world did fall from under me and I'd nothing to stand on or to stand over or to stand for, and I had to rebuild myself, resurrect myself, and in doing so it became clear to me that life is about the three Fs: friendship, fun and freedom. If you have friends, real friends that you can sympathise and empathise with; if you can experience joy in your life – that's what I mean by fun; and if you're free to choose between good and bad, that's what life is about, and this is how I see myself in the community.

My community is an ordinary, exceptionally talented one – there are people in this community who are extraordinarily talented in all aspects of living, and I see my function as somebody who would draw them all together and lead them out. And why do I do so? I do so because I need to. Basically, I'm an educator, and that means educating myself too. Education is a two way process, and, in educating, I need to know that I have people who will listen to me as much as I want to listen to them. As I told you, I started a village festival here some time ago which was very successful. It was a community arts festival, and the reason I wanted it was not for any self aggrandisement, but to know if my potential audience, for my poetry especially, was a real audience, and I found that it was.

*

What does it mean to be a poet in a classroom? It means that, in the same way as in the larger classroom which is the street or the pub or whatever, it means that you can introduce a sense of friendship, fun and freedom:

Friendship – you know the way children are often jealous of each other and are often fighting with each other and all the rest – you can introduce the sense of friendship, that friendship is sharing. It's the big word in the religion programme at the moment, you know: the answer to all questions in religion now is 'sharing', and you can bring that to a far more grounded sense than the easy answer of 'share', 'share', 'share' which probably is only a cliche.

You can bring a sense of fun. Now, classrooms are not traditionally associated with fun, but you can allow people to express themselves, and not just in the traditional programme, the three Rs. I'm not denigrating the three Rs – people have to have them. You can't send out somebody into the world who can't read, or who can't multiply – I mean, I'm very conscious of this, but that's not where the excitement for me is. The excitement for me is allowing people, say in a drama lesson or interpreting a poem or a song, allowing people to create themselves, to say themselves, to speak themselves, to manifest themselves through fun, because fun, you see, isn't idle. When I was in leaving cert. I studied an essay of Robert Louis Stevenson's called 'An Apology for Idlers'. Idling is probably the most creative pastime there is, or activity there is, because it's where you give your mind space. When the mind wanders, if it's in any way a creative wandering, magnificent connections happen, and this is fun, this is what I mean by fun.

The freedom is that they have the right to say to me 'I don't agree with you', 'You think you're the biggest man in the world'.

*

I see what happens in a place like Moyvane: there's a re-creation going on. We're given, we're dealt our cards; the cards of living, the cards of dying – birth, copulation and death as Eliot called it. They're cards of unemployment, they're cards of dole, they're cards of not enough houses to go around, they're all these cards, and the simple thing is, you could just lie down and die – the simplest answer to that is to die, I mean at a spiritual level. But no! the people don't; I mean they say 'No! We can imagine ourselves into a greater truth'. There is a greater truth than the dole, there is a greater truth than unemployment. There is the truth that, no matter what any economic system can do to us, we are ourselves, we are people and we are capable of singing, and saying, and dancing, and thinking ourselves. And this, I think, is what's happening, because the realities of life can be often lousy. Wasn't it Behan who said it: 'Oh death, where is thy sting-a-ling-a-ling? or grave thy victory?' That's the old Christian story. I think we're in a fundamentally Christian society when we can do this, that we can say that life can throw its worst death at us and we can resurrect; that we are powerful and imaginative enough not to die. Isn't that where the Christian story came from, maybe, you know, that we refuse to die?

*

I'm content to put in my time as a teacher, I'm content to learn from the children. It would be a different story if I thought

74

that the adventure had ended; I mean, thanks be to God and touch wood, teaching for me is an adventure. What is it to be a teacher? A lot of teachers, notwithstanding the joy and the adventure, sometimes say 'We're wishing away our lives'. We're no sooner back after Christmas than we're looking forward to the Easter holidays, and we're no sooner back from Easter than we're looking forward to the summer holidays which, of course, is a process of wishing your life away. And then there's also the matter of any young teacher, not just myself, coming with a great vision of how to change society, how to change life, and, I mean, you don't – not even politicians do that. At the same time, if you can connect with children, and sensibilities, if you can connect with sympathy that is beyond attention once or twice in your life (which is all, maybe, that a good teacher can expect) you really influence somebody's life.

*

THE TEACHER

I wish away my life until the pension
Hoping that, just once, I will connect
With sympathy that is beyond attention;
Instead I keep good order, earn respect.
Once I had a vision for my village –
I'd bring to it a gift of poetry;
Tonight the talk's of quotas and of tillage
And how the barmaid gives out beer for free.
And yet, I've not lost hope in my own people –
My vision was at fault; these people need
To sing and dance, get drunk below the steeple
That accuses them of gossip and of greed.
I mind their children, give them right of way
Into a world I've seen and try to say.

21

Poetry and School

Ask most people if they enjoy poetry and they will probably answer no. Yet they will sing songs and buy records (folk and rock music are, after all, a kind of oral poetry), recite dirty ditties, talk of sport in terms of 'poetry in motion' and so on. What has happened? Poetry, for them, is most likely associated with the unpleasant experience of the poetry lesson, the *ceacht filíochta*, at school. Humankind simply cannot escape poetry: it's part of our nature. The problem is, how do we define poetry?

I do not propose to rehearse a popular versus elitist argument here. What I want to say is that poetry, the dialogue of self and soul, is that which most puts us in touch with ourselves. Poetry is concerned with beauty and truth, and each person must find his or her own aesthetic. School can help here. The total experience of school should help each pupil along the way of finding a personal aesthetic. The total experience of the school in its community should lead children to ideas of truth and beauty, the natural corollary of which is their expression in words, images, movement, music, etc. The total experience of school will integrate, not divide, the human spirit, the most perfect expression of which may be referred to as 'poetry'.

As I have suggested, there is poetry all around us. What football team wins a final without wanting a song of commemoration to it? Because the cup, or a medal, is not enough – the stuff of mere mortals perhaps! True immortality is being named in poem or song. Every community has its poets and singers.

They have a function in their society – to tell it as they see it; to show society as it is, or might be. If their poetry is any good, it delights or annoys (usually in the same proportion!), and leads society to reflect upon itself, perhaps thereby to grow, to flourish, to mature.

If there were no schools, there would still be poetry. Poetry wasn't 'invented' in, or for, schools, but to make sayable the human soul. The child's experience of poetry will not begin in school – long before the child becomes verbal, it will invent its own sounds, and combinations of sounds, rhythms and rushes of euphony and discord, a pre-poetry if ever there was one! Later, the child will delight in all sorts of rhymes and verses, for sleep, for play, for social intercourse. So the teacher would do well to realise that children love poetry before they come to school. Perhaps the best we teachers can do is to keep that love alive. Too often we kill it with syllabi and syllables, by measuring instead of treasuring.

Poetry is written to say the unsayable, to sing the unsingable, to make the word flesh. Many pupils instinctively know this (they mightn't be able to say it, but there are more than intimations of immortality in early childhood!).

How can a hard-pressed school promote poetry? First of all, by not compartmentalising the curriculum into pigeon holes of learning – let the curriculum be a continuum, let there be overlap everywhere; let there be respect for words – let there be etymology where appropriate to show how words come about; let there be trust in the classroom; let the pupils voice their honest opinions with respect.

On a more practical level, let the teacher present poetry (and song) that he actually likes and believes in. This will almost certainly involve going outside the poetry in the class reader. Indeed, there is an urgent need for comprehensive anthologies of poetry for Irish schools which contain poetry in English and Irish, the latter with translations where necessary. The divide between poetry in English and Irish as it is sometimes taught in our schools is an unnatural one. Pupils should be allowed to react to poetry – if they don't like it, they shouldn't be forced to pretend they do. They should be encouraged to learn the poems they like by heart. Different kinds of poetry should be presented. Remember that much 'adult' poetry can be presented successfully to the young.

If there is a local poet in the area, bring him/her into the classroom. Let him/her share their poetry and rhymes with the children – thereby showing that poetry happens primarily outside the classroom, and is not written to persecute school-children! Indeed, through the imaginative 'Writers In Schools' scheme, many leading Irish poets and writers can be invited to visit our schools at very little cost to the individual school. Many teachers are availing of this invaluable service.

Children should be encouraged to write poetry. The same applies to children beginning to write poetry as to anyone else: it takes a long time to find out what you have to say, and how best to say it. So, initially, let the writing sprawl and fall if it must. The teacher is a facilitator in this process. He can inspire, encourage, cajole, direct; he cannot ultimately 'correct', because in poetry there is no one 'correct' way: there is only one's own way, and this must be respected.

What are the effects of poetry? Does an aesthetic necessarily become an ethic? I think not. What it does, I think, is that it leads us to ideas of truth and beauty. On the way, it can lead us to an appreciation of language and the process of language; it can elate or depress; it can be a bulwark for the unthinking, trotting out the 'apt' quotation instead of examining the truth. It can become a way of life. Like everything else, it can be good or bad, and it affects us personally and individually. It may never become popular, but it will always be truly of the people.

22

The Listowel Literary Phenomenon

A question that is frequently asked is how is it that the Listowel area in north Kerry has thrown up so many good writers? – writers of the calibre of George Fitzmaurice, Maurice Walsh, Thomas MacGreevy, Bryan MacMahon, John B. Keane and Brendan Kennelly to mention just creative writers. The answers are various – none of them, to my mind, entirely satisfactory. The common answers are that there is a traditional love of learning in the area; that there is a strong classical tradition in the area; that the area is an enclosed, gossipy one with a love of fine words, poetry, song and story; that the people of north Kerry are great talkers; that north Kerry inhabits an area fertilised by two languages (Irish and English). And so on. Certainly all these conditions exist in north Kerry. Or they did up to recently. But the same could be said of many areas. It's a phenomenon I don't understand. Is it just a monumental fluke, or is there something else at work? I honestly don't know. I can only talk from my own experience.

Moyvane, the village where I grew up, and still live in, seven miles from Listowel, was full of songs and stories. There was no television when I was growing up, and very few radios. Very few people read books, but the oral tradition was strong. There was no *seanchaí* in the village, but there were stories and songs, snatches of sporting derring-do, ghost stories to scare us children into staying home at night, stories of *piseogs*, snippets of local history, the lore of neighbours 'rambling' to each other's houses – the first question always asked was 'Any news?' We lived in a strange world halfway between the empirical world of the rational mind and the magical world of superstition. Some of the ghost stories we were told were believed as much by their tellers as by ourselves.

Things 'ran in families': the Cunninghams, my mother's people, 'had brains'. My grandfather, Maurice Cunningham, was a poet. I wasn't aware of that until 1984 when I stumbled across it in a very strange way. My distant cousin, Mary Anne Cunningham (Mrs Ned Liston of Athea, a neighbouring village), a woman of advancing years, called me aside shortly after *Rainsong*, my first collection, was published that summer. She congratulated me on its publication and confided in me that she was glad I was writing poetry. I took it simply as a compliment until I found out her real reason for congratulating me. After my grandfather died, she, alone among the Cunninghams, took up the poet's pen. The *piseog* ran that when the poetry passed to the women of the family, the poetry died out of the family in that generation. I was the next generation. The poetry had passed on.

I remember, too, as a young boy the talk about a new play, *Sive*, in 1960 or thereabouts. Cars were hired to take the 'literati' of the village to Listowel where *Sive* was playing. My father and mother hired a car to take them to see it too. The village was agog with this new play. Stories began to filter through about its author, John B. Keane: he stayed up all night writing; he read books while eating … To my impressionable mind, that was high romance, far away from the reality of surviving in a small village. I wanted that. I wanted people to be talking about me like that. (I would have been about seven at the time!)

And people used to come to our house to talk about literature. My mother had a passion for art – books, paintings, music – and spent much of her time reading when she became invalided with 'heart trouble'. That was before her sight failed. Undaunted, she borrowed 'talking books' from the Society for the Blind, and encouraged me to listen to her favourite classics. I remember, too, a local parish priest who used consult her. He would occasionally present her with a 'doubtful' book (where he got them I'll never know) for her opinion. That's how I first came across *The Country Girls*! My mother gave it to me. And the poor penitent who had confessed to reading it never knew! My mother had the greatest influence upon me. Without her, I wouldn't have become a writer. I deeply regret that she didn't live to see, apart from juvenilia in college magazines, a single line of mine in print.

In north Kerry there's something to live up to, something to pit yourself against, if you're a writer. There's little doubt in my mind that a writing tradition creates writers, as a footballing tradition creates footballers and so on. And there's an audience too. An audience for song and story, poetry and plays. Anywhere there's fine talk, the people of north Kerry will flock to hear it – and put in their own 'spake' too.

It's a matter of awe that the Listowel area has, for well over a hundred years now, regularly produced worthwhile writers, some of them writers of genius. It remains a mystery and, like all mysteries, defies explanation. All we can do is wonder about it. In wonder writing begins …

23

'Missing' the Master

On 18 September 1992, Bryan MacMahon, perhaps Ireland's most eminent schoolmaster, launched *The Master*, his teaching memoirs which was to become a bestseller in Ireland. I wonder why this, and not his collections of short stories which, to my mind, show him at his masterly best, made it to the bestseller list.

For good or ill, people remember their teachers. A teacher, MacMahon has stated, leaves the track of his teeth on his community for three generations (an unfortunate metaphor, perhaps, as teachers are not supposed to bite their pupils!). In *The Master*, MacMahon has provided Ireland with an opportunity of seeing the course of Irish national teaching and the fortunes of its teachers in post colonial Ireland through a teacher's eyes.

MacMahon belonged to a generation which held the schoolmaster in high regard. In rural Ireland, the way out of the poverty trap for a bright boy was through teaching or the Church. Interestingly, the same didn't hold true for girls – teaching, certainly, was an option taken up by many girls, but the Church, namely the convent, meant a vow of poverty. The highest achievers in the leaving cert. tended to take the option of 'the call to training' (to be trained as national teachers) – I belong to the last of those generations, having qualified as a national teacher in 1972. It is inexplicable to me why these high achievers, some of the brightest students in the country, were denied a degree course in the training colleges. We are N.T.s (national teachers): we hold a diploma. The training colleges couldn't provide a degree course, the B.Ed., until 1974. It is something many of us regret, not for the status of having a primary degree, but because a three-year degree course, rather than a hectic two-year diploma course, would have been more enlightened and enlightening, not to say more leisurely – we sat in our lecture halls from 9 a.m. to 5 p.m. or later, five days a week in my time. Crammed with education!

I am grateful for my education. The first teachers I met (in the national school in Moyvane where I now teach) were diligent, fair, erudite and enthusiastic. If, as certain revisionists now claim, the history curriculum we were taught was likely to turn us into little Anglophobes, it had no such effect. I do not, and never have, hated England or the English. The (very few) of our schoolmates who became involved in republican politics came from republican families.

There are no 'schoolmasters' nowadays. The term is obsolete. I'm not a schoolmaster. I'm not 'the master' to anybody in the village. I am generally 'Gabriel' (not 'Gabriel Fitzmaurice') to one and all, sometimes 'Miss' to my newly arrived six-year-olds in first class. This is interesting. 'The Master' has become 'Miss'! Is this why so very few men want to become teachers nowadays? That it is perceived as a woman's profession? That men are afraid to admit the feminine in their nature, all *yang* and no *yin*? That men are afraid to approach women as equals? It is fair to say that a high achieving male student would not nowadays look to teaching as a first option. There is more money, more power, more prestige in other professions. This, I think, would be the perception.

Certainly, the teacher is no longer, with the priest and perhaps the doctor, the most revered and feared person in the community. And no bad thing either. We are what we are. We cannot, and should not, hide behind masks of authority. We should be visible in our communities. The teacher nowadays is liberated in his/her community by this very lack of 'authority'. To work with people as equals brings out the sense of friendship, fun and freedom that enlivens society, that vitalises us. The teacher can still be central to the community. The record speaks for itself. And in the larger community, in the community of Irish life, teachers still play a central role: in Irish letters (Bryan MacMahon, Roddy Doyle, Pat McCabe, Michael Mullen, Michael Coady immediately come to mind); in Irish music (to take just Irish traditional music as an instance, look to the achievement of Máire O'Keeffe, Mairéad Ní Mhaonaigh, Máire Ní Bheaglaoíoch, Iarla Ó Lionáird, Declan Masterson, *et al.*); in theatre (people like Joan Sheehy and Éamon Kelly come to mind); in sport, in broadcasting, in politics, in every field of human endeavour.

A teacher, ideally, is a spiritual leader. He inspires, encourages, cajoles, advises the community to fulfil its promise. When this happens, and these epiphanies are often local, often barely visible, the teacher has achieved his ends.

But the job has its difficulties. Traditionally, the bane of the teacher's life was an inflexible, unimaginative inspectorate which would descend on the classroom like a wolf on the fold. Nowadays, in a more enlightened world, the inspector works hand in hand with the teacher for the good of the child, which is only as it should be. In former times, teachers feared the vengeance of what was, in effect, a thought police: the relentless and often brutal system of examining Christian doctrine. Again, this difficulty has been addressed. The diocesan religious examiners are trained catechists now, and have wide experience in dealing with teachers and children.

Nowadays, the bane of every teacher's life is the type of

solicitor who will take the opportunity to sue a teacher on the slightest pretext. Many teachers live in fear of them. Teachers supervise children in the school playground at lunchtime. They do so at their peril. What teacher can now take a P.E. class without the fear that, in the event of any accident, however small, he will end up in court? Or worse, as happened in one case, to my certain knowledge, when a teacher became aware of an award made against him only through reading it in a newspaper. (This teacher wasn't even informed that the claim against him was going to court). And there are teachers I know who have been threatened that they may be sued if they implement the *Stay Safe* programme aimed at preventing child abuse. There's a lot of fear in teaching nowadays. It's no place for the frail! You have to be tough, you have to be committed, you have to be motivated, you have to have a vision for yourself and your community. Otherwise, you burn out early and can't afford to retire.

24

The Gift of Ink:
The Legacy of Bryan MacMahon

Bryan MacMahon, 'The Storyman', died on Friday, 13 February 1998. It was a sad occasion, the passing of an era; but he had lived to a ripe old age (he was eighty-eight when he died), and had fitted many lives into one lifetime. He was husband, father, grandfather, schoolmaster, ballad-maker, playwright, novelist, translator, lecturer, storyteller supreme. He had said himself among his people, and he passed through the gap of life with dignity.

Bryan MacMahon dominated Listowel like the twin spires of Saint John's and Saint Mary's churches in the town square. You felt his presence as he perambulated Listowel in search of high talk and tall tales. And he found it. Right through his long life he found nuggets on his daily rounds. Nuggets that he would fashion into literature. Here is an example – a litany of answers in reply to his question 'How are you?' put to the oldsters idling in the marketplace:

'What way are you, Paddy?'
In sepulchral tones, 'Perpendicular, no more.'

'What way are you, Jack?'
'Keepin' the best side out like the broken bowl in the dresser.'

'Jim, what way are you?'

'If I felt any better I'd see a doctor.'

'What way are you, Vincent?'

'Stumbling along between the immensities.'

'What immensities?'

'The immensities of birth and death.'

From encounters such as these, MacMahon was to write some of the finest stories to come out of Ireland in the twentieth century.

Yes! Bryan was a schoolmaster, a pillar of society. He had all the *gravitas,* the erudition, the presence to carry it off. But there was a native Kerry *rógaireacht,* a touch of roguery, about him too. Let me state here and now that all great schoolmasters (and mistresses) – the terms are obsolete now – have a touch of roguery. It keeps their pupils interested because, at any moment, magic can happen. Take the case of the elephant. As I recall it, Bryan was in class one day when a circus man came to his door. He came to advertise that his circus would be playing in town that week. Bryan, a twinkle in his eye, enquired: 'Have ye a baby elephant, by any chance, in the circus?' The circus man replied that they had. 'Can you have him outside my door at *exactly* twelve o'clock tomorrow? And can you make sure that you're not seen by the children?' The circus man departed and Bryan returned to his class.

'I can do magic – do you know that?' he smiled.

'What kind of magic, sir?'

'Well, I can make animals appear. Name me an animal and I'll make it appear.'

'A mouse.'

'Ah, no! That'd be too easy – he's too small.'

'A dog.'

'Too small, too small. I'll tell ye – tomorrow at twelve o'clock, just after the Angelus, I'll make an elephant appear.'

And, do you know, the following day at twelve noon, just as he had promised, a baby elephant appeared!

*

Bryan MacMahon was many things in his lifetime. He was a great collector – particularly of folklore and ballads. He travelled the countryside collecting the lore of the old folk of north Kerry – the last native Irish speakers in the area. Later he would mix with the travellers, 'the tinkers', befriend them (at a time when it was neither popular nor profitable), learn their language (which is called 'Shelta' or 'Gammon'), collect their lore and immortalise them in poem, play, novel and story. He began to write his own ballads, ballads of his locality – the tragedies of the War of Independence, the beauty of the River Feale, the magic of the Listowel Races are all chronicled and, more importantly, are still sung. His ballads were printed locally on sheets, really off-cuts from the printing press of his friend, Bob Cuthbertson. He presented and scripted 'The Balladmakers' Saturday Night' on Radio Éireann, our national radio station.

The best ballads go into the tradition and are eventually anonymous. This is happening to some of Bryan MacMahon's ballads – 'The Valley of Knockanure', for instance, commemorating the shooting by the Black and Tans of Paddy Dalton, Jerry Lyons and Paddy Walsh at Gortaglanna, Knockanure, on 12 May 1921. This ballad is sung throughout Ireland. Indeed, Seamus Heaney has reminded me that he used to hear it 'belted out with total conviction at the céilís in south Derry in the 1950s'. And he is 'quite sure that it hasn't lost its popularity in some quarters there to this day'. Outside of north Kerry – where there is some dispute about its authorship! – virtually no one knows who wrote it. Everyone knows that Yeats wrote 'Down by the Salley Gardens' because it is not a true folk ballad; no one knows who wrote 'The Valley of Knockanure' because it is.

Bryan MacMahon was a playwright. Among his plays staged at the Abbey Theatre were *The Bugle in the Blood* (1949), *Song of the Anvil* (1960) which was the Abbey's choice for the International Theatre Festival and included incidental music from Ceoltóirí Cualann under Seán Ó Riada, and *The Honey Spike* (1961, and revived in 1993). He wrote many other plays, both full length and one act, including *The Master* which he would later refashion into a bestselling book of memoirs. These plays have been staged throughout Ireland and their popularity is enduring.

He has also made his mark as a novelist – notably with his first novel, *Children of the Rainbow* (first published in 1952) and *The Honey Spike* (first published in 1967). He has been a translator from the Irish. His translation of the autobiography of Peig Sayers of the Great Blasket Island, first published in 1974 and reprinted many times, is more than a labour of love. It is an act of genius, translating one world, the Gaelic, pre-capitalist, pre-modern world of the Blasket islanders, to the frantic world of the twentieth century. And he succeeds. He translates *Peig* faithfully, closely, idiomatically, lovingly. Unfortunately, and I know Bryan would agree with me here, as people turn less and less to Peig's Irish original, they will have to fall back on Bryan's translation to discover a way of life that survived into the 1950s. But translation is not an ignoble art. It is an act, sometimes, of repossession. And not all the poetry gets lost in the translation! Take, for example, his translation of "Sé Fáth mo Bhuartha', a traditional Irish folksong:

'Tis my bitter sorrow that by tomorrow
I go not out to my true love's bower
Where the stream that's running spills purest honey
And in wintertime see the branch in flower.
No frost, no snowing; no red wind blowing
By the bright abode of my secret queen
But her body moving with the salmon's beauty
And her hair ashine like the barley green.

Oh may God be praised for young women's laughter
Tho' it scald the heart of one grey and cold
And may God be praised for the bitter rapture
That takes my body as in days of old
For Satan has me as a black companion
When I cast my thoughts on what might have been
On her body moving with the salmon's beauty
And her hair ashine like the barley green.

That is a work of beauty, and a joy forever. Though not a replica, it is faithful to the spirit of the original; it is as powerful as the original, the true child of the poet and the translator.

Bryan also wrote for children. I want to comment briefly here on his 'Patsy-O' books and his folk tale *Jackomoora and the King of Ireland's Son*. To be honest, I don't think the 'Patsy-O' books represent him at his best. Once, in an unguarded moment, he told me that he wrote them with his left hand. By which, I suppose, he meant not with the urgency or the passion of his short stories, novels, ballads or plays. The schoolmaster is too much in evidence in 'Patsy-O'. He is inclined to intrude into the narrative, to include an unnecessary lesson (I am thinking, for instance, of the geography 'lesson' in his story *High in the Sky with Patsy-O*). That technique is sound pedagogy – but the

Storyman can do better. And he has – in his folk tale *Jackomoora and the King of Ireland's Son*. Let me tell you how powerful it is.

On the morning of Friday, 13 February 1998, just before I left for school, I was informed that Bryan had fallen into a sort of coma. I decided that I would read one of his stories to my third class (nine year olds). I decided on *The Gap of Life*. My son John thought better. 'Read us *Jackomoora*,' he said. The story tells of Jackomoora and the King of Ireland's son who travel on a quest to the end of the world, an enchanted world, a marvellous world, marvellously realised in the telling. It is a tale that means different things at different levels, like all great folk tales. You could hear a pin drop while I was reading it. The children clapped when it was over.

'Did you like that?' I asked them.

'Yeah.'

'Was it as good as television?'

'Yeah, better.'

'Was it better than *Gigantor*?'

'Yeah.'

'Was it better than *Sonic the Hedgehog*?'

'Yeah.'

'Better than *Star Trek*?'

'Yeah, better. Way better. Way, way better.'

That is the power of story, and Bryan MacMahon was a superb storyteller.

A superb storyteller, Bryan MacMahon looked at the ordinary and saw the extra-ordinary. He will be remembered as a great short story writer. At his best, he wrote brilliantly. But better, he wrote memorably. His first collection, *The Lion Tamer*, was published in 1948. He told me that he had submitted it to the *Kerryman*, a local newspaper that sometimes published books. Having left it to them for more than a year, and having heard nothing from them, he demanded his manuscript back. 'Gabriel,' he fixed me with his eye, 'I decided to take it from the smallest publisher in the world and give it to the biggest!' Macmillan of London published it. His final collection, *A Final Fling*, was published by Poolbeg Press of Dublin in February 1998. Bryan had the pleasure of holding a copy in his hand before he died.

Bryan MacMahon wrote of ordinary things – of love, of families, and tinkers, and teaching, and sports, and fighting, the intercourse of opposites, men and women, the old and young, the Christian and the pagan. Indeed, he described the short story as the mating of a male idea with a female idea – the intercourse of opposites.

*

Bryan MacMahon is the master personified. He lived in an era when the priest and the teacher were feared. Yet he never traded in fear. Instead he opened the windows of wonder. His realm was magic, the magic of words that transform life. All life can be re-created. He re-created himself in fiction whose root, in his beloved Latin, is *fingere*, to form or fashion. He fashioned himself. He fashioned his community. He says it best in *Children of the Rainbow*:

> I consider it the duty of at least one old man in every generation to pass on the ferocity he has inherited. Often an' often I have told ye of the place ye were born into. I have striven to raise in ye a pride for the noble people before ye who fell in love with human nature an' through human nature fell in love with God … I have striven to convey before now that the young life as I lived it was so thronged with small beauties that you wouldn't think 'twas sons

and daughters of the flesh we were, but children of the rainbow dwellin' always in the mornin' of the world … an' if only the All Seein' God had seen fit to send us a man with the gift of ink, then maybe the story of our small wonders would go shoutin' through the borders of the nations.

Bryan MacMahon had the gift of ink. He lived all his life in his native Listowel. A writer of the small town, but not a small town writer, he showed us how to take our place among the nations of the earth. The master is dead. Long live the master.

25

Where History Meets Poetry: Bryan MacMahon and 'The Valley of Knockanure'

> If a man were permitted to make all the ballads, he need not care who should make the laws of a nation.
>
> – Andrew Fletcher of Saltoun (1653–1716), Scottish patriot

According to this reading, we are as influenced by the poetry of a nation as we are by its history, and more so than by its laws. In this light let us consider the ballads of the events of Thursday, 12 May 1921 at Gortaglanna in Knockanure, Co. Kerry.

The months of April and May 1921 saw a lot of bloodshed in the parish of what is now Moyvane-Knockanure near Listowel in north Kerry. This was, of course, during the Irish War of Independence.

On Thursday, 7 April, Mick Galvin, an IRA volunteer, was killed by British forces during an ambush at Kilmorna in Knockanure. The IRA had been lying in wait to ambush a group of British soldiers who were cycling to Listowel after a visit to Sir Arthur Vicars at Kilmorna House, his residence. Vicars had been Ulster king of arms and custodian of the Irish crown jewels which were kept in Dublin Castle. Their burglary, in 1907 – although Vicars was never seriously suspected of being involved in their theft – led to his ruin and, ultimately, to his death.

Found guilty of negligence and dismissed from his post, ruined socially and financially with neither position nor pension, Vicars, at the invitation of his half-brother, George Mahony, came to live in Kilmorna House. When George died in 1912, he left the estate to Sir Arthur's sister, Edith, who lived in London. She decided that Sir Arthur could live out his life in Kilmorna. That he remained there during the War of Independence when British forces and Sinn Féin activists were matching atrocities was foolhardy rather than courageous, and typical of the man who was generally regarded by the local people as a decent, if eccentric, gentleman. But he was also passing information on IRA activity to the British army.

On Thursday, 14 April 1921, Kilmorna House was raided by the local IRA. One of the party, Lar Broder, told the steward, Michael Murphy, that they had come to burn the house, which they proceeded to do. However, three members of the flying column led Vicars to the end of the garden and shot him. (One of his executioners, Jack Sheehan, was subsequently shot dead by the British army near Knockanure on 26 May).

On 12 May, Crown forces shot dead three members of the flying column at Gortaglanna, Knockanure, a short distance from Kilmorna. This is the incident that is commemorated in the various ballads that follow.

Poetry, particularly narrative poetry to which the ballad belongs, distorts historical fact for aesthetic reasons – these may be for the imperatives of narrative, for considerations of rhyme or metre, or for reasons of the poet's perceptions or sympathies. The ballads of the events in Knockanure on 12 May 1921 are no different. No version gets the facts entirely right. All versions tell a basic story but even the most historically accurate distort the facts. Some, either from carelessness or ignorance, or from unrestrained fancy, depart from historical fact entirely.

The most famous ballad of the events is Bryan MacMahon's 'The Valley of Knockanure', written in 1946 – though, in the true spirit of tradition, its authorship is disputed. Let's clear this up immediately. On 16 August 1969, Pádraig Ó Ceallacháin, republican and retired principal teacher of Knockanure national school, wrote the following testimony:

> I, Pádraig Ó Ceallacháin, formerly Príomh-Oide Scoile of Knockanure NS, Co. Kerry hereby affirm that about 20 years ago I brought to Mr Bryan McMahon [*sic*.] NT Ashe St. Listowel a few verses of a traditional ballad on the murdering at Gortagleanna [*sic*.] Co. Kerry in May 1921 of three soldiers of the Irish Republican Army – Jermiah [*sic*.] Lyons, Patrick Dalton and Patrick Walsh. I also supplied Bryan McMahon with a copy of the sworn statement of Con Dee the survivor and requested him to rewrite the ballad and to add whatever verses were necessary so that it would be historically accurate. This Bryan McMahon did and later supplied me with printed copies of the ballad in question 'The Valley of Knockanure' a copy of which is affixed herewith.
>
> Signed: Pádraig Ó Ceallacháin; Date: 16/8/69
> Witness: Aibhistín Ua Ceallacháin

THE VALLEY OF KNOCKANURE (Co. Kerry)
In memory of Jeremiah Lyons, Patrick Dalton and Patrick Walsh,
murdered by Crown forces at Gortagleanna, Co. Kerry on 12 May 1921

You may sing and speak about Easter Week or the
heroes of Ninety-Eight,
Of the Fenian men who roamed the glen in victory or defeat,
Their names are placed on history's page, their memory will endure,
Not a song is sung for our darling sons in the Valley of Knockanure.

Our hero boys they were bold and true, no counsel would they take,
They rambled to a lonely spot where the Black and Tans did wait,
The Republic bold they did uphold though outlawed on the moor,
And side by side they bravely died in the Valley of Knockanure.

There was Walsh and Lyons and Dalton, boys, they were
young and in their pride,
In every house in every town they were always side by side,
The Republic bold they did uphold though outlawed on the moor,
And side by side they bravely died in the Valley of Knockanure.

In Gortagleanna's lovely glen, three gallant men took shade,
While in young wheat, full, soft and sweet the summer breezes played,
But 'twas not long till Lyons came on, saying 'Time's not mine nor your',
But alas 'twas late and they met their fate in the Valley of Knockanure.

They took them then beside a fence to where the furze did bloom,
Like brothers so they faced the foe for to meet their dreadful doom,
When Dalton spoke his voice it broke with a passion proud and pure,
'For our land we die as we face the sky in the Valley of Knockanure.'

'Twas on a neighbouring hillside we listened in calm dismay,
In every house in every town a maiden knelt to pray,
They're closing in around them now with rifle fire so sure,
And Dalton's dead and Lyons is down in the Valley of Knockanure.

But 'ere the guns could seal his fate Con Dee had broken through,
With a prayer to God he spurned the sod and against the hill he flew,
The bullets tore his flesh in two, yet he cried with passion pure,
'For my comrades' death, revenge I'll get, in the Valley of Knockanure.'

There they lay on the hillside clay for the love of Ireland's cause,
Where the cowardly clan of the Black and Tan had
showed them England's laws,

No more they'll feel the soft winds steal o'er uplands fair and sure,
For side by side our heroes died in the Valley of Knockanure.

I met with Dalton's mother and she to me did say,
'May God have mercy on his soul who fell in the glen today,
Could I but kiss his cold, cold lips, my aching heart 'twould cure,
And I'd gladly lay him down to rest in the Valley of Knockanure.'

The golden sun is setting now behind the Feale and Lee,
The pale, pale moon is rising far out beyond Tralee,
The dismal stars and clouds afar are darkened o'er the moor,
And the banshee cried where our heroes died in the Valley of
Knockanure.

Oh, Walsh and Lyons and Dalton brave, although your hearts are clay,
Yet in your stead we have true men yet to guard the gap today,
While grass is found on Ireland's ground your memory will endure,
So God guard and keep the place you sleep and the Valley of
Knockanure.

It's clear from this that the words we now sing, whatever about their ancestry, are Bryan MacMahon's.

Let us compare this, the best version, and closest to historical fact, with the actual history of the event as given first hand by Con Dee, the survivor of the atrocity:

SWORN STATEMENT ON THE INCIDENTS AT GORTA-GLANNA MADE BY CON DEE BEFORE THOMAS R. HILL, J.P., TARBERT, IN JUNE 1921

About nine-thirty a.m. on Thursday, May twelfth, 1921, I Cornelius Dee, accompanied by Patrick Dalton and Patrick Walsh [Dee's first cousin], left Athea unarmed, where we had been attending a mission given by the Redemptorist Fathers. We were walking along the road leading to Listowel when at Gortaglanna bridge we met Jerry Lyons; he was cycling. He dismounted and began talking about various happenings. After a few minutes Paddy Walsh suggested that we should go into a field as it would be safer than the roadside. We moved and were just inside the fence when we heard the noise of a lorry. 'Take cover, lads,' I advised, and we tried to conceal ourselves as best we could. Jerry Lyons, Paddy Dalton and I took cover immediately. Paddy Walsh ran to the end of a field and lay down. Very soon we were surrounded by men in the uniforms of the Royal Irish Constabulary. 'We are done, Connie,' said Paddy Dalton. 'Come out, lads,' I said, 'with our hands up.' Jerry Lyons, Paddy Dalton and myself stood with our hands over our heads. Paddy Walsh ran towards us. We were met with a torrent of abuse and foul language. I remember such expressions as 'Ye murderers', 'Ye b-------', 'We have got the real root', 'We have got the flying column'. We were asked our names and gave them correctly; we were searched and found unarmed, having nothing but a copy of the *Irish Independent*.

We were then compelled to undress and while we were fastening our clothes again we were beaten with rifles, struck with revolvers and thrown on the ground and kicked in trying to save ourselves. Then we were separated some distance from each other; four or five men came round each of us and my captors continued to beat me with their rifles and hit me with their fists. After about twenty minutes we were marched towards the road and then to the lorries. Paddy Walsh and Paddy Dalton were put in the first lorry. I was put in the second, and Jerry Lyons in the third. The lorries were then driven for about a half a mile towards Athea. They were then stopped and turned round. Paddy Walsh and Paddy Dalton were changed to the lorry in which I was. Jerry Lyons was not changed out of the last lorry, which was now leading. The lorries were then driven back the same road for about a mile. We were then ordered out of them.

I looked at my companions; I saw blood on Jerry Lyons' face and on Paddy Walsh's mouth. Paddy Dalton was bleeding from the nose. We were then asked to run but we refused. We were again beaten with the rifles and ordered into a field by the roadside. We refused but were forced into the field. We asked for a trial but the Black and Tans laughed and jeered and called us murderers.

We were put standing in line facing a fence about forty yards from the road. I was placed first on the right, Jerry Lyons was next, Paddy Dalton next, and Paddy Walsh on the left. Then a Black and Tan with a rifle resting on the fence was put in front of each of us, about five yards distant. There were about ten more Black and Tans standing behind them. I looked straight into the face of the man in front of me. He delayed about twenty seconds as if he would like one of his companions to fire first. The second Black and Tan fired. Jerry Lyons flung up his arms, moaned and fell backwards. I glanced at him and noticed blood coming on his waistcoat; I turned round and ran. I was gone about twelve yards when I got wounded in the right thigh. My leg bent under me, but I held on running although I had to limp. I felt that I was being chased and I heard the bullets whizzing past me.

One of the lorries was driven along the road on my front and fire was maintained from it. After I had run for about a mile and a half I threw away my coat, collar, tie and puttees. The Tans continued to follow me for fully three miles. When too exhausted to run further, I flung myself into a drain in an oats garden. I was there about forty-five minutes when two men came along. They assisted me to walk for about forty yards. I was limping so much that one of them sent for a car and I was taken to a house.

I recognised Head Constable Smith, Listowel, along with the Black and Tans present at the massacre; also Constable Raymond, and there was one in the uniform of a district inspector of the Royal Irish Constabulary.

The official report issued on 14 May 1921 from the Dublin Castle publicity department reads as follows:

> Three RIC tenders were ambushed by about 100 armed men at Kilmorna near Listowel at 1.15 p.m. on Thursday (May 12). Two RIC were slightly wounded. The dead bodies of three unknown rebels were found at the scene of the ambush, and it is believed they suffered heavy casualties. Crown forces also captured a number of shot-guns, revolvers and ammunition.

Years later, in 1958, Con Dee was to revisit the tragedy in an article he wrote in *The Shannonside Annual*. In it, he tells us that, owing to an outbreak of scabies, or 'IRA itch' as it was called at the time among members of the north Kerry flying column, in early May 1921, it was decided to disperse the flying column in groups of three or four to get medical treatment. Paddy Walsh, Paddy Dalton and Con Dee consisted of one group. Paddy Walsh insisted that the three go to his home in Gunsboro in the parish of Ballydonoghue, 'the hub of activity for north Kerry' according to Con Dee. This they did.

Shortly afterwards, Dee writes in that article:

> A volunteer by the name of Buckley from Listowel came to Walsh with a dispatch, which stated that a conversation of a certain woman in Listowel with the police was overheard by a barmaid. The woman told the police that a mission was being held in Athea, and that it was more than likely that the west Limerick column would be attending devotions there. She also said that she would get all the information she could from a friend of hers who had a religious goods stand at the mission. When I relayed the message to the others, we decided under no circumstances would we let the west Limerick column be trapped. We agreed that Paddy Dalton

[a native of Athea] and I should proceed at once to Athea.

Dalton and I decided we'd make faster time if we travelled without arms. We felt time was of the utmost importance to fore-warn our comrades. We travelled by way of Tullamore, Knockanure, along the river Gale to Kilbaha, where we stopped at Hanrahan's and had some refreshments. We continued along the river as far as possible, and then cut across and arrived in Athea about three o'clock in the afternoon.

We visited our good friend, Josie Liston, and told her our mission. She immediately got in touch with the west Limerick column and local volunteers. That evening we contacted the local mailman and made arrangements to meet him next morning to censor the mail.

[Dee and Dalton went to the devotions in Athea] for at no time at all [Dee continues] did any of the fighting men miss an opportunity to attend church if at all possible. After devotions Patrick Dalton and I visited the Fathers who were staying at Danaher's Hotel. We told them also of our mission. They became angry to think such a thing could happen, and wanted to have the woman put out of the village right away, but we objected as we figured we might get some information from the mails. We attended devotions for three nights and visited the priests until eleven o'clock each night ...

Paddy Dalton's home was about a mile from the village and each night we went there. I well remember the first night we were go-ing home, when we were a short distance from the house, Paddy remarked that the family was still up. I asked him how he knew, he remarked that they were looking at the cattle. Again I asked, 'How do you know?' He replied, 'Don't you see the lights in and out of the cow house?' I did not see the light. When we got to the house we went to his father's room and asked him if he had been out. His father replied, 'No'. He then went to the other rooms and asked his brothers. He received the same answer, 'No'. The next morning we got up early and while at breakfast started to discuss the lights of the night before. No one paid much attention to it, but Paddy himself.

The routine the next night was the same. We went to devotions, visited the priests and started for home about the same time. The same thing happened. Paddy again saw the lights, but I did not. He again questioned his people, but they again replied that they had not been out with a light. He wasn't satisfied till we went out and looked all over. We could see or hear nothing and went to bed.

The next day we were joined by Patrick Walshe [*sic.*] in the village. We again attended the mission, went to confession, visited the priests and left for Paddy's home.

Again when approaching the house, Patrick Dalton and Patrick Walshe both saw the lights. I didn't see them. When the family was again questioned, they replied the same as the two previous nights. This time the two Patricks went out and searched but found nothing. The next morning the lights were again discussed. It was passed off as a joke. This was Thursday, 12 May.

Now let us consider some other ballads of the atrocity. J. Anthony Gaughan in his book, *Listowel and its Vicinity*, prints MacMahon's ballad almost verbatim but omits verses two ('Our hero boys they were bold and true ...') and eight ('There they lay on the hillside clay ...'). He changes the line 'And side by side they bravely died in the Valley of Knockanure' to 'And side by side by side they fought and died/In the Valley of Knockanure'. He changes the order of two of the verses – he has the verse beginning ''Twas on a neighbouring hillside/We listened with calm dismay' preceding the verse beginning with 'They took them then beside a fence/To where the furze did bloom'. (MacMahon has them the other way around – which makes narrative sense).

The Clancy Brothers and Tommy Makem Song Book includes a much truncated, though essentially Bryan MacMahon's, version of 'The Valley of Knockanure'. Historical inaccuracies creep in: 'They rambled to a lonely spot where the Black and Tans did hide' (the Tans did not hide, they happened upon the Gortaglanna martyrs); as in Gaughan's version above, they carry the line 'And side by side they fought and died in the Valley of Knockanure' (they did not fight – they were captured unarmed); 'But e'er [*sic.*] the guns could seal his fate, young Walsh had broken thro'' (it was Dee who escaped), and 'The summer sun is sinking low behind the field and lea' (it should be 'Feale and Lee', two local rivers). This displays a lack of knowledge of local history and geography, understandable in the mutating nature of a folk ballad, but historically inexcusable.

Another version of Bryan MacMahon's ballad was recorded by Paddy Tunney, the renowned Irish traditional singer on his *Ireland Her Own* LP. It is published in *Irish Writing in the Twentieth Century: A Reader* edited by David Pierce. It is, in the opinion of Pierce, 'one of the best songs composed about the War of Independence in 1919–21. Listen to Paddy Tunney singing this on Topic Records and you can hear the heartbeat that accompanied Ireland in its transition from colonial rule to independence'.

It is, once again, factually inaccurate. It states, once again, that 'side by side they fought and died/In the valley of Knockanure'; that the event took place 'Upon an autumn evening' (it did not – it was the morning of 12 May); that they were waiting 'upon a brief dispatch/To come from Tralee town' (they were not – note Tim Leahy's ballad below); that 'As Dinny spoke his voice it broke' (there was no Dinny present on that day); that 'The glistening stars shone out afar/And gleamed o'er Collins moor' (there is no such place in Knockanure); that Dalton 'fell in the fight' (there was no fight); lastly, it makes no mention of Con Dee's escape. Here is Paddy Tunney's version:

THE VALLEY OF KNOCKANURE

You may sing and speak about Easter Week
And the heroes of '98,
Of the fearless men who roamed the glen
For victory or defeat.
There were those who died on the green hillside
They were outlawed on the moor;
Not a word is said of the gallant dead
In the valley of Knockanure.

There was Dalton, Walsh and Lyons boys,
They were young and in their pride.
In every house in every crowd
They were always side by side.
The republic bold they did uphold
Though outlawed on the moor,
And side by side they fought and died
In the valley of Knockanure.

Upon an autumn evening
These three young men sat down
To wait upon a brief dispatch
To come from Tralee town.
It wasn't long 'til Lyons came on
Saying time isn't mine nor yours
But alas it was late when they met their fate
In the valley of Knockanure.

Upon a neighbouring hillside
We listened in calm dismay,
In every house for miles around
A maiden knelt to pray.
They're closing in around them now
With rifle-fire so sure,
And Dalton's dead and Walshe [*sic.*] is down
In the valley of Knockanure.

For they brought them hence beyond the fence
Wherein the furze did bloom,
Like brothers now they faced the foe
To meet their vengeful doom.
As Dinny spoke his voice it broke
With a passion proud and pure:
'For our land we die as we face the sky
In the valley of Knockanure.'

There they lay on the damp cold clay
Martyred for Ireland's cause
Where the cowardly clan of the Black and Tans
Has showed them England's laws.
No more they'll feel the soft breeze still
Or uplands fair and pure
For the wild geese fly where the heroes lie
In the valley of Knockanure.

When the evening sun was sinking
Beyond the Feale and Lee
The pale moon was rising
Way out beyond Tralee.
The glistening stars shone out afar

And gleamed o'er Collins moor,
And the banshee cried where the heroes died
In the valley of Knockanure.

I met with Dalton's mother
And these words to me did say:
'May the Lord have mercy on my son
Who fell in the fight today.
Could I but kiss his cold cold lips
My aching heart would cure,
And I'd gladly lay him down to rest
In the valley of Knockanure.'

Now, apropos that final verse: there is a tradition in and around the parish of Athea, bordering Knockanure, that the 'original' version of 'The Valley of Knockanure' was written by James Kiely Mahony, from Knocknaboul, Athea. This tradition has been conveyed to me by: Donie Lyons, an All Ireland senior singing champion from Glin, a neighbouring parish in west Limerick; Domhnall de Barra of Athea, singer, musician and former president of Comhaltas Ceoltóirí Éireann; and Dan Keane of Moyvane-Knockanure, a poet and All Ireland senior champion composer of Newly Composed Ballads at Fleadh Cheoil na hÉireann – all men of unimpeachable integrity. No one now seems to know what Kiely Mahony wrote. It is possible that he wrote an early version, now lost. Dan Keane states in his book *Around Athea* (2005) that a Mrs Hartnett of Abbeyfeale, a daughter of Kiely Mahony, confirmed to him that her father wrote 'The Valley of Knockanure', that she remembered him writing the line 'I was speaking to Dalton's mother'. Be that as it may, there is no doubting Bryan MacMahon's authorship of the ballad as attested in Pádraig Ó Ceallacháin's testimony.

The spalpeen poet, Paddy Drury (1859–1945), a native of Knockanure, wrote a number of ballads about the atrocity. One of his versions, 'The Dawning of the Day', is less a narrative of the events than a vehicle for his own anti-English, pro-de Valera, anti-Treaty sentiments. Though it is not possible to date its composition, it clearly originates from a time when 'Kerrymen are fighting still' before de Valera, as leader of the IRA, can say 'lay down your guns, the fight is won', and before the same de Valera, as taoiseach of the Irish Free State government in the early 1940s, executed Kerrymen Maurice O'Neill of Caherciveen and Charlie Kerins of Tralee for IRA activity:

THE DAWNING OF THE DAY

O, Holy Ireland, suffering still,
Your troubles now are great,
From tyrants trained to shoot and kill
Whose minds are filled with hate;
Who sold their souls for foreign gold
To rob and steal away;
It's no wonder that our hearts are sad
At the dawning of the day.

Sons of north Kerry, proud and true,
Step forward every man;
You know the foreign bloodhound crew,
The murderous Black and Tan
Who shot young Lyons and Dalton
And Walsh the proud and gay
As they left their gallant comrades
At the dawning of the day.

On Gortaglanna's rugged height
Surrounded by that crew
How could they stand, how could they fight,
What could our martyrs do?
They showed no fear when death was near,
When the tigers sought their prey,
But our blood ran cold when the tale was told
At the dawning of the day.

But Kerrymen are fighting still
From Dingle to Tralee;
I'm proud to be a Kerryman
And I'm proud of sweet Athea;
I'm proud of Lyons, that noble lad
Who gave his life away
As he left his gallant comrades
At the dawning of the day.

When writing down the Roll of Fame
In old Ireland's history,
With green and gold illume the name
Of gallant brave Con Dee;
I'd give my life to clasp his hand
And 'tis with him I would stay
And fight by his side for my native land
At the dawning of the day.

The above is the version given by Jeremiah Histon in his article 'I Remember Paddy Drury' printed in *The Shannonside Annual* of 1957. Jack Carroll of Listowel, a respected traditional singer and a reliable source of local ballads, had the following concluding verse which I collected from him in the 1970s:

Oh Mother Ireland, dry your tears
Be ever full of cheer,
Pray for those noble volunteers
Who fought to set you free.
When freedom comes to Ireland's sons
De Valera* he will say,
'Lay down your guns, the fight is won
At the dawning of the day'.

In politically sensitive company, Jack would change the de Valera reference to:

When freedom comes to Ireland's sons
Brave Irishmen will say,
'Lay down your guns, the fight is won
At the dawning of the day'.

Another of Drury's versions goes as follows:

THE GLEN OF KNOCKANURE

May the Lord have mercy on their souls,
Their hearts were loyal and true,
They were beat and shot in a lonely spot
In a glen near Knockanure.

There was Jerry Lyons, now, from Duagh,
There was Dalton from Athea,
There was Walsh from Ballydonoghue
And Con Dee who ran away.

Through hill and vale he did leg bail
As the bullets pierced the ground

Till he jumped the stream at the Bog Lane
Where he blinked the devil's hounds.

Through mountainside he did tide
Though wounded then and sore
And he shed a tear for his comrades dear
Who were bleeding in their gore.

For our martyrs bold, now dead and cold,
To the lorries were thrown in
And Smith* said there was an ambush at
The Gortaglanna glen.

For now Sinn Féin prove that you'll gain
And remember those who died
And let each man try to keep his eye
On Smith* and on McBride*.

Now we have two more we sad deplore
That in this parish fell,
They are Galvin and Sheehan.
In Heaven they all dwell.

Smith and McBride were two of the Black and Tans/RIC who were present at Gortaglanna on that day.

Tim Leahy of Mount Rivers, Listowel also made a ballad. His version, composed on 20 September 1921, is printed in Colm O Lochlainn's *More Irish Street Ballads* first published in 1965.

This is a faithful version of the events at Gortaglanna. What it lacks in drama and personality, it makes up for in local detail, details that other versions don't give us – for instance, he tells us that the boys were coming from mass that morning, that they were waiting for a dispatch (there is no evidence of this in Con Dee's testimony nor is it mentioned by Danny MacMahon, who was working close to his home in Gortaglanna on that day, in his account of their capture published in J. Anthony Gaughan's *Listowel and its Vicinity*); and Leahy alone tells us that they were shot near an ancient ringfort which, incidentally, is still to be seen in front of the ditch where they were shot and where now stands the monument erected to their memory by the north Kerry Republican Soldiers Memorial Committee in 1949. Here is his ballad:

THE VALLEY OF KNOCKANURE

It was in the year of twenty-one,
All in the month of May,
Some of our noble Column boys
Were strolling on their way.
They came from mass that morning,
Their souls were now secure,
But little they thought that they'd be shot
In the Valley of Knockanure.

On a bridge near Gortaglanna
Those boys a rest did take;
They were waiting a dispatch to say
What move they were to make;
With feelings strong to move along
And make themselves secure –
But it was their lot that day to be caught
In the Valley of Knockanure.

Now when those boys were taken,
They were beaten black and blue;
Into the lorries they were thrown –
Alas! What could they do?
They dare not ask for mercy now
But they prayed they might endure
Their torments for their Motherland
In the Valley of Knockanure.

Those heroes' names I'll now relate
Who were captured on that day:
Paddy Walsh and Jerry Lyons
And Dalton from Athea;
Con Dee from Ballylongford
He surprised the Tans I'm sure
When he made that dash for liberty
From the Valley of Knockanure.

Near an ancient fort those boys were shot
And there their bodies lay
Till Ireland's sons a tomb will raise
To them some future day.
So pray the Lord may grant them rest,
Their souls with him secure,
For a martyr's death those heroes met
In the Valley of Knockanure.

What woe and grief to parents came
That night when told the tale
In every house they knelt and prayed
Along the River Gale
For those gallant boys who gave their lives

Our freedom to secure
And relieve Con Dee that wounded be
In the Valley of Knockanure.

And now to the version where history and poetry part company
entirely, the version recorded from Joe Heaney (Seosamh Ó
hÉanaí) by Ewan MacColl and Peggy Seeger in their home
in Beckenham, Kent, England in 1964. Joe, by way of giving
background information, has the following to say:

> You know in Ireland every six months, the priest comes around to
> give advice and confessions to the old people, you see, in the cot-
> tages. And there's one particular house they come to every time.
> Well this day they came to Knockanure in County Kerry and it was
> in 1922 and there was two wee lads, Éamonn Dalton and Danny
> Walsh was on the run up in the hills and five lorry loads of Black and
> Tans came to hunt them. And they had a boy, a fourteen year old boy
> called Con Dee bringing them messages to tell them how the Tans
> was behaving and the Tans, fifty Tans, [a] hundred Tans, I should
> say, surrounded them with rifles and they told Con Dee to get away
> somewhere and bring a message to the village that they were willing
> to die to save the village. And the two fellows died. But the people,
> the old people coming, as they do there, they come along, old wom-
> en and men and to spare them, the two lads fought to the death with
> a hundred Black and Tans up on the hill and saved the village from
> ruin, because if they ran back to the village, the lads were afraid the
> Tans would come back and probably kill innocent people.

And he sings:

You may boast and speak about Easter Week
Or the heroes of ninety-eight,

Of the gallant men who roamed the glen
To victory or defeat.
The men who died on the scaffold high
Were outlawed on the moor.
Not a word was spoken of two young lads
In the Valley of Knockanure.

'Twas on a summer's evening
Those two young lads sat down.
They were waiting on a brief dispatch
To come from Tralee town.
It wasn't long till Lyons came on
Saying 'Time's not mine nor yours,
Look out we are surrounded
In the Valley of Knockanure.'

Young Dalton grabbed a rifle
And by Walsh's side he stood.
He gazed across the valley
And over toward the hill.
In the glen where armed men
With rifles fired galore,
There were Dalton, Dan and the Black and Tans
In the Valley of Knockanure.

One shot from Dalton's rifle
Sent a machine gun out of play.
He turned to young Lyons and said
'Now try and get away.
Keep wide of rocks, keep close to nooks
And cross by Freeney's moor,
And Danny and I will fight or die
In the Valley of Knockanure.'

The summer sun was sinking fast
On Kerry by the sea.
The pale moon it was rising
Over sweet Tralee.
The twinkling stars they shone so far
Out on the dreary moor,
And when Dalton died, the Banshee cried
In the Valley of Knockanure.

God bless our bold Sinn Féiners
Wherever they may be.
Don't forget to kneel and pray
For that hero brave Con Dee.
He ran among the Kerry hills
To the rich man and the poor,
Salt tears he shed for those he left dead
In the Valley of Knockanure.

Our hero boys were stout and bold,
No counsel would they take,
They ran among the lonely glens
Where the Black and Tans did lay,
The women of the uplands
Gazed out across the moor
Watching Dalton and Dan fighting fifty to one
In the Valley of Knockanure.

And 'twas God who sent those boys to life
But did not say how long,
For well we knew that England's crew
Would shoot them right or wrong.
With our rifles fixed right up to fire

And bullets quick and sure,
We'll have revenge for those young men
In the Valley of Knockanure.

Young Éamonn Dalton and Danny Walsh
Were known both far and wide,
On every hill and every glen
They were always side by side.
A republic bold they did uphold,
They were outlawed on the moor,
And side by side they fought and died
In the Valley of Knockanure.

I met with Dalton's mother,
Those words to me did say,
'May the Lord have mercy on my son,
He was shot in the getaway.
If I only could kiss his cold, cold lips
My aching heart would cure
And I'd lay his body down to rest
In the Valley of Knockanure.'

This has more to do with Hollywood than history and it calls into question the great singer's authority in matters historical. It calls into question, too, the historical authority of folk song. Basically, as we all know, song is not history. Nonetheless, Joe Heaney's version demonstrates how history becomes legend. And we need legend. Though historically inaccurate, legends are true to the spirit of their people, that indefinable coming together of historical fact, memory, story, song and poetry that make us what we are.

Nowadays, the events of April and May 1921 are almost

entirely forgotten, even in the parish of Moyvane-Knockanure where they occurred. Galvin, Vicars, Dalton, Lyons, Walsh, Dee and Sheehan are scarcely remembered. Some may welcome this amnesia as a good thing. But amnesia is never good. We forget our history at our peril. We censor our poetry to our cost. Let a poet have the final word. Art Ó Maolfabhail, writing in his poem 'Inis Córthaidh agus Gné den Stair', about Enniscorthy and the events of 1798, states that 'ní mór peacaí ró-ghránna/ na staire a mhaitheamh' ('the ugly sins/of history must be pardoned').

We must forgive history's ugly sins. But to forgive them, we must first know what they are.

26

Sive

John B. Keane was born on 21 July 1928 in Listowel, a busy market town and capital of north Kerry. He was born into a rich literary tradition. For centuries the O'Connors of Carrigafoyle and the Fitzmaurices of Lixnaw, the principal families of the area, had been generous patrons of the arts. Later Pádraig Liath Ó Conchubhair, born 1745, poet and schoolmaster, presided over a bardic school in Lisselton some four or five miles from Listowel. Later still, George Fitzmaurice the playwright, born in Listowel in 1877, Maurice Walsh the popular novelist, born in Ballydonoghue just outside Listowel in 1879, Thomas MacGreevy the poet, born in Tarbert some ten or so miles from Listowel in 1893, and Bryan MacMahon the celebrated short story writer, novelist and playwright born in Listowel in 1909, kept the tradition alive as would Keane and his near contemporary, Brendan Kennelly, who was born in 1936 in Ballylongford, some eight miles from Listowel. Along with the high literary tradition of the area, there was a rich vein of oral poetry where local rhymers, some of them illiterate, would praise and excoriate as the occasion demanded. Indeed, this indigenous rhyming tradition continues to this day.

Keane was educated locally in Listowel national school; his father was an assistant teacher when the four year old John B. entered the junior infants class. (The following year, his father left to take up the post of principal teacher in Clounmacon national school, some three miles from Listowel.) On leaving the national school, John B. entered Saint Michael's College, also in Listowel, a junior seminary with a strong tradition in the classics; Latin and Greek being compulsory subjects there. John B., something of a rebel even then, was expelled several times for smoking, speechmaking, ballad-writing and play-acting. One incident left a lifelong mark on him. One day in May 1947, in an elocution class, the boys were asked to recite a few stanzas from a suitable poem. When it came to Keane's turn, he recited 'The Street', a poem he had composed himself (and which he would later publish, in 1961, in the eponymous collection). The teacher asked him who had composed the poem. When John B. informed him that it was his own composition, he was severely beaten and ejected from the class. He left Saint Michael's with an honours leaving certificate at the second attempt.

On leaving Saint Michael's he worked at various jobs – as an assistant, for instance, to a fowl buyer, and as an apprentice to Keane-Stack's chemists in Listowel. On 6 January 1952, he emigrated to Northampton, England, where he worked in a chemist's shop, and later as a street cleaner for the corporation. He endured the corporation for two months during which time he wrote a short novel in the Patrick MacGill style which was rejected by no fewer than eight publishers. Having left the corporation, he worked for British Timken, an Anglo-American steel company. Eventually, he left Northampton and worked as a barman in Leicester and London.

However, after two years working in England, he returned to Ireland and got a job as a chemist's assistant in Doneraile, Co. Cork, where he wrote another novel which was also rejected. Then, having spent one year in Doneraile, he returned to Listowel, bought a pub and, on 5 January 1955, married Mary O'Connor, the love of his life. He lived happily with Mary in Listowel thereafter.

Keane from early on had an interest in the theatre. As a teenager, he and his brother, Eamonn, who would later become a renowned actor, would write and stage their own plays in Listowel. Indeed having met with local success – for which read having made some money out of it! – the young John B. Keane founded his own theatre company which he mischievously titled 'The Willie Brothers'. Their performances included singing, dancing, fortune-telling, and a succession of sketches and one-act plays written by John B. About this time, too, he was having some of his poetry published in local and daily newspapers.

His three-act play, *Barbara Shearing*, was accepted by RTÉ for broadcast on radio. According to John B., 'it was only a diversion and it lacked depth'. Before it was broadcast, however, he and his wife went to see the Listowel Drama Group in Joseph Tomelty's *All Souls' Night*, the first full-length play of consequence he had seen up to then. When he got home, bursting with creative energy, he sent Mary up to bed, filled a pint for himself, and had the first scene of *Sive* written by 6.30 a.m. The year was 1958. *Sive* was rejected by the Abbey Theatre, but took the country by storm when the Listowel Drama Group staged it in 1959. It won the premier award at the All Ireland Drama Festival in April of that year. Ironically, the Listowel Drama Group would become the first amateur group to stage a play in the English language under the auspices of the Abbey Theatre when they packed the Queen's every night for a week during a sultry week in May 1959.

If the play was an unqualified popular success, it was not, however, an unqualified critical success. Critics pointed to weaknesses in the text: faulty curtain lines, the contrived letter scene, the melodramatic ending. But that is what it is, a brilliant melodrama. Keane never wrote for critics. A writer and publican in a rural town, he knew his audience. He knew the power of theatre, how by its language and passion it can command attention. In *Sive* he took an old folk tale, a stock dramatic situation (the forced marriage of a young woman to an old man), and revived it by the power of his language. This is the heightened language of the Munster poets of the Hidden Ireland where what is lacking in intellectual quality is more than compensated for by its turbulent moods and passionate language. *Sive* is a melodrama in the very best sense. Keane used everything he had learned from the productions of his teenage years which were as influenced by the music hall and the variety concert as by any of the Greek, Latin, English or Gaelic texts he studied in Saint Michael's College. Indeed the two tinkers, Pats Bocock and Carthalawn, his musical son, in commenting on the action of the play, perform the function of the Choruses he met in the Greek plays he studied there. Keane studied the Greek play, Euripides' *Iphigenia in Tauris* for his leaving certificate in Saint Michael's, and would have been aware of the Greek Chorus, an awareness he brought to his writing of *Sive*.

But I have already alluded to the rhymers indigenous to the area who had the power to curse and bless at their pleasure. This function of the poet in Ireland is an ancient one, and the local rhymers, though far removed from the high poets of antiquity, reserved the privilege, indeed the right, to praise or curse in their verses. Consider one such rhymer, Paddy Drury (1859–1945), a native of the Bog Lane in Knockanure just outside Listowel. (Incidentally, John B. was one of the instigators of a project to erect a headstone over Drury's grave in Knockanure as Drury died destitute.) Drury, though illiterate, had the power of his craft. He could extemporise to devastating effect. Here he is in semi-jocose mood castigating a farmer's table for the poor quality of its fare:

May the Lord above look down with love,
Have pity on us four,
And give us *mate* [meat] that we can *ate* [eat]
And take away the boar!

This sharp wit, which Keane had in abundance, Carthalawn displays when he comments on the action in *Sive*. Thus, the rhyming tradition of the indigenous, illiterate *spailpín* poets influenced Keane, and is more than a little responsible for the character and songs of Carthalawn, himself such a poet.

If *Sive* is a melodrama, it is also a play of genius full of brilliant insights into the rural life of its time. It is 'the changing of the times', as Pats Bocock, the poet Carthalawn's father, proclaims. It is a time when the old, traditional ways are being supplanted by the new Ireland where people are being school-educated and money is becoming more plentiful.

The play examines issues like illegitimacy and childlessness, both taboo subjects in the older Ireland. It was a primitive, brutal, patriarchal society where to have no father (that is, to be born illegitimate) was to have no rights. Hence, Mena, the young Sive's sister-in-law, realises that from a social and economic point of view, the match between Sive and the old man, Sean Dota, with the grass of twenty cows and the holding of money, is a good match for the illegitimate Sive.

In such a society, the holding of money is power. Mena knows this. She knows that the power of money can find its way even into the confession box where 'the black sins in your soul will be laughed away because you are rich'. But Sive has convent education – she has book learning, she reads poetry. Her husband-to-be, Sean Dota, typifies a local understanding of poets: 'I have nothing against the poets, mind you, but they are filled with roguery and they have the bad tongue on top of it, the thieves,' he exclaims. Sive is of the new, emerging Ireland; 'She has book learning', her brother Mike, Mena's husband, tells us. Because of this, she is different to Mike and to the traditions he stands for where matchmaking is necessary in country places. 'She will turn a deaf ear to matchmaking,' he laments.

If illegitimacy is taboo, so too is childlessness. In a patriarchal society, succession is everything. A father must have sons to carry on his name, to farm his few acres. Daughters are secondary to this to be used as society decrees. (Of course one might point out that the sons, also, are victims of this process, and are used equally for the 'good', if such it is, of that society.) Childlessness is shameful. And it is always the woman who is blamed for this childlessness – never the man. Mena is childless and is despised by her mother-in-law, Sive's beloved grandmother, for this.

This is a world where the love of husband and wife is unspoken. In a society where love is looked upon with suspicion, where love can thwart the matchmaker (who is the personification of patriarchy), demonstrations of love are frowned upon. 'In the name of God, what do the likes of us know about love?' the matchmaker asks rhetorically. 'Did you ever hear the words of love on his lips,' he asks Mena, referring to her husband. 'He would sooner to stick his snout in a plate of mate and cabbage, or to rub the back of a fattening pig than whisper a bit of his fondness for you … Could you say that he ever brought you the token of a brooch or a bit of finery? … Naa. More likely a few pence worth o' musty sweets if the drink made him foolish of a fair day. And to hear you bladderin' about love! The woman would think you were out of your mind if you put a hand around her on the public road,' he taunts, adding later 'what business have the likes of us with love? It is enough to have to find the bite to eat.'

This is the disappearing world that John B. captures so

powerfully in *Sive*. If he recognises the necessity of the new Ireland, he is sympathetic to the older traditions too. (Maybe this is where his true sympathies lie – not to the cruelties of the time but with the people who had to endure them). Though not condoning the selling in marriage of the young girl to the old man, he understands and sympathises with the people who are forced by economic imperatives into such a contract.

One feels that the Ireland of the Celtic Tiger is totally out of sympathy with such a society. A society of mobile phones and plastic money is light years removed from patriarchy and poverty. Yet, I feel, *Sive* speaks no less powerfully to the society of the Celtic Tiger. It speaks in the blood, in the primal, primeval recesses of the human psyche. There is a Sive and a Mena in all of us.

Sive is a play for voices. It depends on its language; the musical inflection of his native north Kerry is heightened to poetry. In this, his language can be compared to George Fitzmaurice's. In their hands it is a language that not only aspires to, but achieves, the condition of music. *Sive* has been broadcast a number of times on RTÉ radio. From its first broadcast, by the Listowel Drama Group in May 1959, it has been obvious that *Sive* makes great radio. Radio depends on the human voice. Radio is, especially, a language medium. It appeals to the ear and to the imagination. It brings us visions on the air. Thus *Sive* in its richness of language and simplicity of plot, is ideal for radio. If it verges on the sentimental, it doesn't drown in sentimentality. Full of sentiment, it demonstrates, to quote Robert McDowell, the American poet and publisher, that 'sentimentality is borrowed emotion … [S]entiment is just that emotional response the situation calls for, and … is all one's own.'

Sive set rural drama alight; it is a landmark in Irish folk

126

theatre. Despite its harshest critics, it made Ireland wake up to its indigenous culture, a way of life that had been ignored or maligned by the emerging new Ireland of the 1950s and 1960s. It has stood the test of time. It has had revivals in the theatres of the cities, including Dublin, and is regularly performed by rural drama groups in village halls, community centres and pubs.

Throughout his career, John B. Keane was always his own man. He kept faith with his own people, finding in them originality and genius, qualities he brought to the wider world in his plays, stories and poems. He has been an example to the next generation of north Kerry writers, myself included. Far from the centres of culture, he, like his fellow townsman Bryan MacMahon, demonstrated that the writer of genius can turn the commonplace into a centre of the imagination.

27

Beating the Goatskin till the Goat Cries: the Importance of Folk Song and Music to John B. Keane, the Man and Playwright

North Kerry is rich in folk song and music. If its singing and music traditions are eclipsed by the more famous north Kerry writers, it is because many of these writers have drawn on these traditions and made them new. Bryan MacMahon wrote 'The Valley of Knockanure' and many other ballads of enduring popularity; Brendan Kennelly wrote in his poem 'Living Ghosts' of singers who 'in their innocence/[are] Untroubled by right and wrong./I close my eyes and see them/Becoming song'. But the point isn't that MacMahon made ballads or that Kennelly appreciated singers. The point is that many of the north Kerry writers used the song and music traditions of the locality to create their own art.

Ballads are the oral history of a people; if not always strictly factual, they present their story as it might, or even should, have been. Ballad singers and local musicians traditionally gathered in the kitchens of local 'rambling houses' where to 'ramble' meant no aimless wandering but to go to the rambling house for conversation, music, song and dance. In later times when the rambling houses declined, they 'rambled' to the local pub. One such pub was John B. Keane's in Listowel.

John B. Keane was a Listowel man. A 'Townie'. 'Townies'

and 'Country Mugs' are natural enemies. But in his youth John B. Keane summered in the country – in Lyracrompane among the Stacks mountains between Listowel and Tralee. He knew the countryside and its people. He understood them and their customs – their elemental music, their matchmaking, their pagan wells, their pagan fires and rituals. He learned their speech, the authentic north Kerry dialect used for the first time on the Abbey stage in the plays of George Fitzmaurice. He learned their stories. He sang their songs.

So much for tradition. John B. Keane could have remained a fine ballad singer, respected among these people. But he had ambitions towards being a writer: he would re-make that tradition, he would make it new. And he did in plays like *Sive* and *Sharon's Grave*, plays that looked back to a dark and pagan past; and in *Many Young Men of Twenty* and other plays of emigration where he used the ballad-makers' art to enhance his narrative.

Sive, first performed in 1959, is the timeless story of a young maiden betrothed to an old man. This practice is, the play sings to us, an offence against nature. The singer is not one of the settled people, not one of us. He is a tinker, an outsider, an artist who has the power to curse or bless. The tinker Carthalawn plays, Keane tells us in his stage directions, a 'tambourine'. The tambourine was an ancient goatskin drum. The round, wooden rim was sometimes inset with the flattened metal tops of beer bottles which rattled in sympathy to the rhythm being played on the skin. Unlike the bodhrán, its more refined cousin of today, the tambourine was the instrument of the outdoors, of Wrenboys and Strawboys, the relic of a pagan Ireland. The best players 'beat the goatskin till the goat cried', a phrase much used by them to describe their vigorous, elemental percussion. 'In the distance', the stage directions tell us, 'but ever increasing is the sound of a tambourine and a voice singing. The sound increases while the occupants of the kitchen await Pats Bocock and Carthalawn. The air of the song is that of "'Neath the Bright Silvery Light of the Moon'"– the Irish ballad, not to be confused with "By the Light of the Silvery Moon", the American ballad. The words of the song are impromptu and created by Carthalawn.' Here they are. He begins with a greeting and a blessing on the house:

> Oh! Mike Glavin, you're the man;
> You was always in the van;
> With a dacent house to old man and gorsoon;
> May white snuff be at your wake,
> Baker's bread and curran-y cake
> And plinty on your table, late and soon.

Carthalawn continues by cursing Tomasheen Seán Rua, the matchmaker who arranged the wedding of Sive to the old man, Seán Dota:

> May the snails devour his corpse,
> And the rain do harm worse;
> May the devil sweep the hairy creature soon;
> He's as greedy as a sow;
> As the crow behind the plough;
> That black man from the mountain, Seáneen Rua!

Then Carthalawn alludes to the wedding of Sive: the buying of Sive by the old man:

> On the road from Abbeyfeale,
> Sure I met a man with meal,

'Come here,' says he, 'and pass your idle time';
On me he made quite bold
Saying the young will wed the old
And the old man have the money for the child.

Again Carthalawn curses the matchmaker:

May he screech with awful thirst
May his brains and eyeballs burst
That melted amadaun, that big bostoon,
May the fleas consume his bed
And the mange eat up his head,
That black man from the mountain, Seáneen Rua.

Sive, in desperation drowns herself rather than marry the old man. The final words are left to Carthalawn:

Oh, come all good men and true,
A sad tale I'll tell to you
All of a maiden fair who died this day;
Oh, they drowned lovely Sive,
She would not be a bride
And they laid her for to bury in the clay.

The tinker's singing punctuates the narrative. It comments and curses. It set the audiences of the 'new' Ireland of the 1960s alight. That 'new' Ireland endeavoured to forget its pagan and poverty-stricken past. Keane shoved their noses in it with his tinker's song. John B. knew his tinkers as he knew his country folk. He served them both in his pub. He collected lore from them. Indeed, people felt that John B. got much of his material from the drinkers who frequented his bar. As one of them memorably commented to him: 'Keane, you're a cute man. You takes down what we says and you charges us to read it!'

One of the tinkers whom John B. befriended was Jack Faulkner, a musician and singer. They shared an interest in folk song and music. But on one particular evening when Faulkner arrived for a pint in John B.'s pub, he found his host engrossed in a book. The tinker sipped his pint in silence for a long time until he could take the silence no longer. 'What's that you're reading?' he enquired of Keane. 'It's a long poem called "The Islandman" written by Brendan Kennelly,' Keane replied. Faulkner laid his pint down on the counter and solemnly pronounced: 'John B., poetry is bad enough without it being long.' I tell this story not only as an anecdote but to show how north Kerry feels about poetry. Coming from an oral, singing tradition, we will tolerate poetry only if it sings to us. Keane knew that, Kennelly knows that; I know that and it informs our art.

John B. Keane identified with the tambourine people. Over the course of time, the pagan tambourine became the modern bodhrán. I remember seeing the word 'bodhrán' for the first time on the first Planxty album in 1972. He promoted the local bodhrán makers Sonny Canavan of Dirha Bog and Davy Gunn of Duagh. His first novel, published in 1986, was a homage to *The Bodhrán Makers*, for which read the people of the bodhrán living 'at the bottom of the hills, on the verge of the bog', people like the country folk he summered with as a boy in the Stacks mountains and who he would later welcome to his pub.

John B. wrote other songs and poems. He published *The Street and Other Poems*, the only book of poetry that was to appear during his lifetime, in 1961. The title song from *Many Young Men of Twenty*, his play of emigration first published in 1961, he later refashioned for the Irish tenor Michael O'Duffy in the version that is popularly sung by folk singers throughout

Ireland today. He wrote 'The Buck Navvy Song' recorded as 'Cricklewood' by Christy Moore on *The Box Set 1964–2004*. In the booklet that accompanies *The Box Set*, Christy writes the following note to the song: 'I learned this from Tony Grehan in Moss Side Manchester in 1967. I recorded a poor version on my deleted first album in 1968. I thought to do a simple rendition for this project as a small salute to the recently departed John B. His work will long outlive the names of those who rejected it. I met him twice briefly, each time a great pleasure.' 'Sweet Listowel', his hymn to his native place has been recorded, with the theme from *Sive*, by John B. himself on the CD *Mickey McConnell live at John. B. Keane's*. In composing his hymn to his native place John B. Keane follows a noble tradition common in Ireland and, in doing so, he complemented that jewel in the crown of Listowel: Bryan MacMahon's ballad 'My Silver River Feale'.

John B. Keane loved to sing. He sang ballads, local songs, popular songs, parlour songs. He had a particular affection for racy local ballads such as 'The Road to Athea', the tale of an amorous encounter between a young man and woman on the road to Athea (pronounce 'Athay') in west Limerick. Here is Con Greaney's version of the last verse of that ballad:

We retched [we arrived] in Athea at a quarter to one
And up to the clergy we quickly did run,
'Twas there we got married without much delay
And we broke a spring bed that same night in Athea!

Every Sunday night in John B.'s pub was singers' night. Old timers like his great friends Jack Leahy of Knockanure and Maurice Stack of Cahirdown led the singing. Traditional ballads blended with the songs of Thomas Moore, Percy French and

Phil Coulter, for John B. was no die-hard purist. He was a man who loved a good song, a good tune. He drew on the local song and music tradition and re-created the native, the indigenous for the wider world. In doing so, he was faithful to the native and indigenous. He didn't distort, he didn't take the thirty pieces of silver that, I fear, some of our younger playwrights may have done in their distortions of rural people and rural life.

The elemental ferocity of Carthalawn's tambourine is now lost to the refinement of the modern bodhrán. I once heard a bodhrán virtuoso described in the following way by an old time practitioner: 'Listening to him playing is like listening to a man beating a flour bag.' No one now beats the goatskin till the goat cries. It is again, like it was in *Sive*, 'the changing of the times'.

28

John B. Keane: A Personal Perspective

'There's enough lies written on the headstones of Ireland without my adding to them,' Big Maggie admonishes us in the play of the same name. There's a danger that John B. Keane is becoming a lifetime in its own legend. I don't intend to add to the legend. I come to praise John B. Keane, not to bury him in sentimentality or whimsy.

I got to know John B. personally about 1973 – around the time I severed my connections with the Pioneer Total Abstinence Association and joined the Arthur Guinness Appreciation Society. Having had ambitions towards being a writer (a poet if you please!), I frequented John B.'s pub in hopes of meeting the great man: to meet, perchance to talk; to talk perchance to disclose my ambitions. But, too shy and backward, I never got around to it.

Later, in 1982, in my capacity as chairman of Writers' Week, Listowel, I had the pleasure and the privilege of working with John B. during his first presidency of Writers' Week. It was then that I made bold enough to disclose my literary ambitions. John B. listened with sympathy. He didn't cuddle and muddle with vague encouragement and empty praise. It was clear that if I wished to pursue a literary career, I would have to be determined to the point of obsession and thick skinned as a jockey's genitals. Then there was the matter of talent. That would have to be honed and fine tuned in the school of experience and hard knocks. Could I take it? That was the question.

Fast forward to Writers' Week 1984. *Rainsong*, my first slim volume, was to be launched there. Brendan Kennelly, a great, gentle and wholehearted encourager, had written a short introduction praising my 'easy skill' in a book that was 'lilting [and] lyrical', and which would 'bring a lot of pleasure to a lot of people'. John B., launching the book, took a different tack. In acknowledging what he perceived to be a genuine talent I had for poetry, he said that, for me to develop as a writer, a hard frost would have to develop along the river. (His metaphor referred to the River Annamoy which flows below Moyvane, and which features in *Rainsong* as a source of inspiration and enlightenment.) It wasn't what one expects to hear at a launch. It wasn't what I expected (or, for that matter, wanted) to hear. But it was exactly right. John B. read me well. He knew that I needed a hard dose of reality; that the usual effusions of the book launch could divert me from my real purpose; that false praise could ruin me as a writer. (He knew also, of course, having received bad reviews himself in his early career, that I would need some toughening up in case I suffered the same fate. I did!) He wasn't prepared to mete out false praise; he wasn't prepared to lie. No! He took me on as a genuine writer and he treated me as such to the point of criticising my book at its launch. Could I take it? He would not be disappointed.

Ten years later, in 1994, John B., always an admirer of formal verse, particularly the sonnet, instigated a sonnet competition at Writers' Week. It was a gesture of Yeatsian proportions – 'Irish poets, learn your trade' was the challenge Keane threw down to Irish poets, particularly poets of my generation (and younger), who were producing free verse, much of it forgettable.

I took up his challenge. I started writing sonnets, surprised that I could control the form and say what I needed to say; surprised at how the form actually contributed to the utterance giving it a force and memorability that free verse could not. When, in late October 1994, I sent John B. ten sonnets which I dedicated to him, he immediately replied: 'Dear Gabriel, Many thanks for the ten sonnets. Better than a cheque in the long run and a great beginning to any day. Sincerely, John B.' I had come a long way in his estimation from ten years previously.

Much has been written and said in praise of John B. Keane since his death. His plays have been revived, his books republished. Radio and television broadcasts have been transmitted. In my own way, I was moved to commemorate him. I'm glad it took the form of a sonnet. I think John B. would not be displeased.

IN MEMORIAM JOHN B. KEANE

New Ireland holds you were of Ireland Past,
An Ireland that was changing as you wrote,
That you didn't move with Ireland that was fast
Changing from the times we took the boat
To be Paddies in an England where we'd slave
For a bedroom and a few pints down the pub;
Ireland of the navvy is in its grave,
We've money now where once we used to sub.
'He didn't move with Ireland': let those who
Follow fashion take thought for today;
As Ireland lost its past, a poet, you knew
The timeless things: you wrote them plot and play.
You didn't move with Ireland. No! you stayed
With the primal heart where all true drama's played.

29

The Passing of an Era

I first met Con Greaney in 1975. I had been looking for a song, 'The Rose of Newtownsandes', and had searched high and low for it. Donie Lyons, the singer and musician from Glin, Co. Limerick just over the border from Moyvane, told me one evening that a man called Con Greaney from the parish of Athea had it. I arranged to travel with Donie to Con's house in Rooska in the west Limerick hills.

On the appointed night, Donie and I stocked up with six-packs of Guinness and a noggin of whiskey and travelled to Con's house. We were heartily welcomed by Con and his wife, Kathleen. We left that night with 'The Rose of Newtownsandes' and a tape full of Con's songs. I immediately knew that I was privileged and honoured to have met Con. I knew instinctively that I was in the presence of a genius. But as the years went by and I got to know Con more and more (until indeed he was more like a brother to me than a friend) I knew that I was lucky to have met him. Lucky to have met a man whose likes we'll never see again. When I phoned Tony MacMahon on the evening Con died (22 June 2001), Tony lamented that with the passing of Micho Russell and Con Greaney an era had passed.

When we launched Con's first commercial recording in 1991 (he was then seventy-nine years old), Tom Munnelly, the great folklorist and song collector, launching the tape in Windle's pub in Carrickerry, said that people today are mistaken in thinking that in some golden age of Irish culture, singers like

Con Greaney abounded. He emphasised that singers of Con's genius are unusual, even unique, and always have been. For Con was unique in style and in repertoire. Indeed he could be said to have been the *genius loci*, the presiding spirit, of his locality, allowing the collective genius of the area to flow through him as he poured it forth in song.

Con was a man of irrepressible spirit who lived for singing. When his beloved wife died, and later when his brother Joe died, Con in dejection confided to me that he didn't think he would ever sing again. But Con was never one to wallow in dejection or self pity. Life was to be celebrated and Con was nothing if not a celebrant. Needless to say, Con sang again, and continued singing even on his death bed. The night before he died he sang 'Paddy's Green Shamrock Shore' and a couple of verses of 'Red Haired Mary' for his friend, the musician and singer, Donie Nolan. Even on his deathbed, Con's irrepressible good humour couldn't be extinguished. The Saturday before he died, I called to see him in Saint Ita's in Newcastlewest. I had been told that he was dying. When I went into his room, Con stirred. 'Hello, Con!' I greeted. 'You're looking good.' Con looked up at me with a wry smile and quipped in a weak voice, and with his irrepressible good humour: 'You could be looking good and you going to the other side!'

Con was a generous man. He gave everything he could give: himself, his talent, his time. Indeed to be in Con's time was to be in a kind of after hours (and they often were in the pub!) where the clock's time didn't matter. Con's time was not the clock's time. He didn't live in temporal time. His time was musical time which was all the time in the world.

I'm glad that his last ten years were good to him. His performances filled concert halls, public houses and recording studios from Dublin to Ventry (where Páidí Ó Sé is a particular

139

fan), from Carlow to Cúl Aodha, to Ennistymon and Milltown Malbay. He could fill the largest pub with his presence. I remember one night in Páidí Ó Sé's pub in Ventry, Con was invited to sing a few songs on the Céilí House programme for RTÉ Radio 1. The cream of musicians were sitting in a circle doing what musicians do – playing their hearts out for each other and for anyone else interested enough to listen. Some paid them scant attention. Con was having none of it. A commanding presence in any company, when it came to his turn to perform he stood, all six-feet-plus of him, and opened up into 'Nancy Hogan's Goose'. The entire bar fell silent, hardly daring to breathe as Con held them spellbound while he sang.

Professor Augustine Martin, no mean singer himself, was an admirer of Con's. At University College Dublin (where Con's singing of 'My Cock Crew' grew to cult status among Gus' entourage), Gus used to opine that Con had the larynx of a bull. To which I say that if Con could make a big sound, he also had the subtlety of the true artist. To hear Con sing, to listen to his way with a musical line, to hear his ornamentation of that line was to hear a Seamus Ennis or a Leo Rowsome on the uilleann pipes. Never a prima donna, Con persevered in his art through times when it was neither popular nor profitable.

I will miss him greatly. He is a loss to the whole community of singers and musicians throughout the land and beyond. To paraphrase *An tOileánach*: '*Ní bheidh a leithéid ann arís*'. We won't see his likes again.

30

'Muse, I Claim Your Attention': Celebrating Kerry in Song

Kerry has produced many fine poets/songwriters in the Irish language. One thinks affectionately of Eoghan Rua Ó Súilleabháin (who wrote in Irish and English, though his English work, such as it is, lacks the substance of his work in Irish); Muiris Ó Céirín who wrote *An Spailpín Fánach;* Tomás Rua Ó Súilleabháin of *Amhrán na Leabhar,* and many others whose songs are still part of the folk repertoire today.

In passing, it must be said that, as a general rule, the great folk songs in Irish are of a higher literary standard than many of their cousins in English. The reasons for this are obvious. The Gaelic poets, though their tradition was in decline by the nineteenth century, came from a high literary tradition, were skilled poets in their first language (Irish), and Irish is more amenable to the pyrotechnics of internal rhyme and assonance than English. Their English language counterparts were, at first, working in a language they were none too skilled at using, and were endeavouring to recreate the sound and form of Gaelic song in English. There are, however, some notably successful attempts – one thinks of 'The Boys of Mullaghbawn' with its heavy assonance:

> On a Monday morning *early* [pronounced 'airly']
> As my wandering steps did *take* me
> Down by a farmer's *station*

141

His meadows and green lawn,
I heard great *lamentation*
The small birds they were *making*
Saying 'We'll have no more *engagements*
With the Boys of Mullaghbawn'.

… or Bryan MacMahon's 'The Valley of Knockanure' with its internal rhymes:

You may sing and *speak* of Easter *Week*
And the heroes of ninety-eight,
Of the Fenian *men* who roamed the *glens*
In victory or defeat:
Their *names* on history's *page* are told,
Their memory will endure,
Not a song was *sung* for our darling *sons*
In the Valley of Knockanure.

It is tempting to postulate that as the poets become more familiar with, and confident in their use of, English, the literary standard of their songs improved. What can be said is that a number of fine songwriters emerged, and that their work can hold its own with the songs of the earlier Gaelic tradition. Of course, here and now, it must be stated that a folk song is not a literary text. It is a living entity – subject to mutations depending on the mood and genius of the community and, ultimately, of the singer. Thus the words turn up in different places, in different languages, in different settings. This is as folk song should be if it is to remain alive and vibrant. But, as I was saying, bad English is bad English! In the case of the most successful songs, good English is palpably not the King's, nor the Queen's, English, nor even standard Hiberno-English

– whatever that is. In the best ballads, the language has a flavour and character all its own.

Lamentably, so many ballads are marred by sentimentality. Thus the subject matter – emigration, love, political affairs – is frequently trivialised. Robert McDowell, the American poet and publisher, has differentiated between sentimentality and sentiment thus: 'Sentimentality is borrowed emotion, what we may draw from other writers or the experience of others to mask an inadequate emotional response; sentiment is just that emotional response the situation calls for, and it is all one's own'. The best ballads are full of sentiment, and do not trivialise their subject matter: anger is real anger, love real love. One has only to compare *Dónall Óg* …

> Do bhainis soir díom is do bhainis siar díom,
> do bhainis romham is do bhainis im' dhiaidh díom,
> do bhainis gealach is do bhainis grian díom,
> 'S is ró-mhór m'eagla gur bhainis Dia díom.

> (You took my east and you took my west,
> you took before and after from me,
> you took the moon and you took the sun,
> and I greatly fear that you took my God.)

… with any of the sentimental whinges of the lesser songwriters with their cheap pathos, pious platitudes, and limp aspirations to realise this.

The process of composing local songs and ballads is still ongoing. The tradition survives. Kerry retains a place for its ballads. A local singer, the very 'heart' of the tradition, can, even yet, come into the pub and sing a local, or other, ballad and be heard. In an age when the soporific rhythms of the muzak played at weekends in pubs and lounges throughout Ireland is overwhelming, it is encouraging to see that the same people who imbibe the banalities of the weekend will come along to singing sessions and 'Irish nights', often held in the selfsame venues as the muzak, to listen to reels and jigs, to traditional, and newly composed, songs and ballads.

Traditional songs, sung unaccompanied, require a high degree of skill to be sung properly. The traditional singer takes an air and interprets it in such a way that no two verses are sung alike. There are differences of nuance, of ornamentation, of pace, of phrasing, even of the melodic line on occasion, all depending on the creativity and imagination of the singer.

Popular ballads do not require the same level of skill. Anybody with a robust voice and an ear for music who can sing with feeling and in tune can acquit themselves well here. The better ballad singer will incorporate, where appropriate, some of the techniques of the traditional singer to enhance their performance.

Genteel songs are sung mainly by singers with 'quality' voices, such is the parlance of the day. These voices are not necessarily more cultured than the traditional singers', but display perhaps a different understanding of music and singing. Some exceptional singers, however, are versatile enough to be equally at home in all three categories.

An interesting aspect of traditional singing is that, in general, there are no strictly 'men's' songs and 'women's' songs. Thus Jimmy Crowley, say, can quite sincerely and unself-consciously sing 'The Bantry Girls' Lament', lamenting Johnny's voyage to fight the King of Spain, and Stella Randles can quite authentically sing 'The Boys of Barr na Sráide', a celebration of manliness. Though some songs might be faintly sexist, there is no sexism when it comes to singing them!

It is important that these songs are brought to the boys and girls of Kerry to enable them to hear their own songs sung by their own people. There is, of course, something of a local *pietas* in this, but we do so in the full knowledge that not to know one's own songs, like not knowing one's own language, is a tragedy that can be avoided.

31

Approaching Pentecost: Poetry in Contemporary Society

In ancient Ireland, the poet was one of the most powerful people in society. He had a public function: not only was he a poet trained in the most rigorous of disciplines, he was also, as Professor Bergin wrote in 1913, 'an intellectual aristocrat … a public official, a chronicler, a political essayist, a keen and satirical observer of his fellow countrymen'.

Later, Shelley would term poets 'the unacknowledged legislators of the world'. All societies have, at all times, felt the call of poetry. All societies have, at all times, had poets who have occupied a central position in the imagination of their people. Can we honestly say that this is so in modern society? How many people can today recite one line of contemporary verse? How many of those same people can recite large chunks of poems learned at school? In Ireland, it seems to me, the answer to the second question is almost none; to the third, quite a lot.

This raises the question: *how come?* Why are people who can, and often do, recite poetry virtually ignorant of contemporary poetry? Firstly, it must be stated that the obvious pleasure they derive from their remembered verses (whether the actual memorisation was a pleasure is quite another matter) is reflected in their recitation. Simply, the poems and verses were memorable. By *memorable* I mean that they fulfilled two conditions – they had something to say, and it was well said.

Let me digress here a moment. I am a primary teacher who has been teaching young children for more than twenty-five years now. I am also the father of two young children. I have been watching the way language develops in children with a keen, indeed almost obsessive, interest for years. Children hear the music of language before they attach a particular meaning to a particular word. Meaning for them derives from sound. Sound for them is meaning. It is not yet formulated, and thus limited into words – the children are, as yet, unbroken on the bit of language. Here are two short poems I wrote about some of my son's very early manifestations of language awareness. As we know, in the English speaking world, a child usually pronounces 'da-da' first and follows shortly afterwards with 'ma-ma'. Soon after my son John pronounced 'da-da' and 'ma-ma', he began to show signs that he understood his name; but the first time we knew for sure that he was aware of language was when he obeyed a command.

Language, we all know, has had its imperative uses since earliest times. Indeed Adam's first response to the imperative of language was to acquiesce. Adam was a-moral in Paradise, deserving neither the Creator's approval nor disapproval. Only by becoming immoral, so to speak (by disobedience), could he aspire to the higher morality whereby he could choose God. An unfree choice is no choice. Only by disobeying God's word could Adam begin to choose Him because Adam didn't know good from evil until he ate of the Tree of Knowledge of Good and Evil. So, if our first manifestation of language awareness is to obey its imperative, we must eventually refuse that imperative and, in so doing, discover the freedom of the word. Anyway, in baby talk in Ireland, hands are 'handies' and the command to clap hands is pronounced 'clap handies'.

APPROACHING PENTECOST

Five seasons into language
And Babel's not the same
Pronouncing 'Mama', 'Dada';
You recognise your name.

Babbling to your Pentecost,
You hear and understand –
The first sign is obedience:
Clap handies, John! Clap hands!

So my son showed that he understood by clapping hands. But that is not all. Later it became clear that he did not know the word 'hands' (i.e. 'handies'); it was the *sound* he responded to. At the beach one day, he clapped his hands (clapped handies) when I said that his nappy was 'sandy'. *Sandy* rhymes with *handies*. He heard the rhyme and obeyed its command.

HEARING THE RHYME

You hear
– Not words
But rhyming sounds
And you obey the rhyme,
Clap handies to my 'sandy'
As I learned at the beach …

Here
Language is a symphony
Where you pick up the rhyme,
Where things are sounds
And names are sung
And nothing is defined.

Again, in my years of teaching young boys and girls, I have found that a young boy or girl will not differentiate between song and poem. A child will offer to sing a song and instead will recite a poem, and vice versa. The divide between song and poem is an unnatural one. Children love words for their sound as much as for their meaning. The notion of *one word, one meaning* is anathema to a child (and, indeed, to many poets as well). '"When I write a word," Humpty Dumpty said … "it means just what I choose it to mean – neither more nor less",' Lewis Carroll informs us in *Through the Looking Glass*. So language is an adventure, a discovery, evolving from *words as anything I choose them to mean* to the relative objectivity of the adult's vocabulary. The poet explores this territory between where words can mean anything one chooses them to mean, and where any given word has multiple, or even contradictory, meanings. He brings those words to poem-freedom where they can be read and interpreted at several levels, each layer yielding up its own particular treasures. Babel is fulfilled by Pentecost: the languages of division are reconciled by a language that is capable of being interpreted by all.

To return to my original question – how is it that many people who delight in verse are ignorant of contemporary poetry? Can it be that schools, by presenting and sanctioning a particular type of verse, admittedly delightful and memorable, are conditioning their students, blinding them to the joys of contemporary poetry and art? I don't know. But the purpose of an education is to provide students with a foundation which will enable them to grow. As the Buddhist proverb has it, a pupil must climb on his master's shoulders. Education systems, no matter how enlightened, tend to stifle adventure and curiosity in the interests of conformity. In my own case, I was lucky as I had a classical education which was as good as a dictionary to me; a mother who took me in hand herself to complement my schooling with her passion for music and literature; and a wayward streak that was going to go its own way no matter what. My way was poetry. Zen Buddhism recognises many ways to self discovery: *Gado* (the way of painting), *Shodo* (the way of calligraphy), *Jindo* (the way of philosophy), *Judo* (the way of force), and *Kado* (the way of poetry). My way was *Kado*.

This is the real force of poetry in the modern world – as a way to self discovery. If I don't know myself, I can know nothing. If I know nothing, I can do no good. Here I betray my own concern. I distrust the impersonal, material world of the technocrat. I listen to their language and am frightened. *Product* to the technocrat is not *pro-ducere, to bring* or *lead forth; manufacture* is not *manu-facere, to make by hand.* These words have taken on a dehumanising, even anti-human, aspect where one can no longer say *laborare est orare: to work is to pray.*

How can a poet survive in such an environment? Can a poet contribute to this society?

It appears to me that, unless a miracle happens, and we can never rule out that possibility, poetry cannot be of central importance in a society that respects neither humans nor the word. Our task as poets is to educate society, to reclaim our lost vocabularies, to frame new symmetries. So it is not surprising that more and more poets, believing in the human spirit, have become teachers. Here is the last place on earth, outside of family, religious orders, politics or journalism, where one can influence people and, through them, society. Through the gates of sound and sense, let us enter the mystery of language. Let us make our own noise, and allow others to do likewise. 'In the beginning was the Word,' Saint John instructs us. In making our own noise, in saying ourselves, we are flesh becoming word. Notwithstanding that we are also what we dream, we exist in language; we are because we speak; we are what we speak.

32

'Becoming Song': Brendan Kennelly
– a Ballylongford of the Heart

Brendan Kennelly was born in Ballylongford, County Kerry, on 17 April 1936, the son of Tim Kennelly, publican and garage proprietor, and his wife, Bridie Ahern, a nurse. Ballylongford is a small village like the other villages in the hinterland of Listowel in north Kerry. To understand Kennelly and his poetry, you have to come to terms with the traditional culture of north Kerry – its sports, pastimes and lifestyle – which Kennelly has translated into poetry that is both intimate and epic.

The area is flat land touching both the River Shannon and the Atlantic. It was, in Kennelly's youth, mainly a farming community – mixed farming, milch cows, pigs for the table and for commerce, poultry likewise, tillage (potatoes, cabbage, turnips, carrots and parsnips for the table, mangolds for the animals). The farmers, small farmers mostly, were generally not well off. But they loved to sing. At night they'd go to the local pub on bicycles or on foot (this was before the general availability of the car), drink 'small ones' (whiskies) and pints of Guinness, and swap stories, news, songs and 'recitations'.

Memory, in particular the poet's memory, gathers these moments together. Kennelly's was, and remains, a public house. Brendan heard these songs, stories and recitations regularly in the pub; not just imported songs (from the gramophone and radio – there was as yet no television) but local ballads too,

'Charming Carrig Isle' and others. Later the young poet would make his own ballads. Later still, the mature poet would write affectionately of this in his poem 'Living Ghosts':

> … men in their innocence
> Untroubled by right and wrong.
> I close my eyes and see them
> Becoming song.

Three elements which largely constitute the mystical body of Kerry are football, politics and religion. Indeed, it is often said that football (Gaelic football, at which Ballylongford excels) is the religion of Kerry. A small boy in Ballylongford dreams of playing for his parish – to don the blue-and-white of Ballylongford is to become flesh of your tribal soul, the incarnation of your native place. Brendan Kennelly became flesh of his native place – he played for his street, his parish, his county. He was a very good footballer: to have played minor, junior and senior football with Kerry, as he did, is a distinction achieved by few. But Kennelly came from a family of footballers; all six boys (including Alan, who now runs the pub and garage, John, a priest, Paddy and Kevin, both teachers) played for their county at minor, junior or senior level, while one, Colm, won senior All Ireland football medals with Kerry in 1953 and 1955. The Kennellys were robust footballers when football was a robust game. Brendan was the gentle one.

Football in Kennelly's time was an epic affair. While all the villages belonged to the mystical body of Kerry (which they passionately believed, and still believe, in), they were tribal, too. When Ballylongford took on Tarbert, the neighbouring village, war was declared. Tarbert, the neighbour, is the old enemy. I once asked Kennelly why he hadn't included Thomas

MacGreevy, the modernist poet, born in Tarbert, in his *Penguin Book of Irish Verse:* no doubt he had his reasons, but the one he gave me, half jokingly, was 'MacGreevy was a Tarbert man!'

Football then, especially, had an epic, mythical quality. The game originated from *caid* which was played between two parishes, starting midway between the two, with the winner the team that carried the ball into the opponents' parish – hence the phrase, until recently used in local derbies: 'we bate 'em home.' This was the game where the playing field was invaded regularly by spectators, men and women, and a glorious fracas would ensue, a fracas that would end as suddenly as it began as passion, sated, spent itself. John B. Keane tells the story of a rainy day on a waterlogged pitch when a player was sent off in a north Kerry derby for the 'attempted drowning' of an opponent! Football was, and is, larger than life.

Ballylongford men, as I've said, were, and are, superb foot-ballers. At their best, they play thoughtful, skilful football with a quiet passion. Kennelly was a half-forward – a winger. He liked playing there. It gave him scope, he could create out there, away from the centre of things. The centre players, backs, midfield and forwards carried the responsibility of the game; the winger could create on his own – now in the thick of things, now in space, observing, calculating, now receiving the gift of a ball passed to him, now passing it on, defending, attacking according to the flow of the game. This early involvement in football epitomises Kennelly the poet.

*

After football, politics came next. North Kerry is a republican country. During the Long Kesh hunger strikes of 1981 in which Bobby Sands, and others, died, there was a black flag on every telegraph pole from Tarbert to Tralee. In the struggle for independence (1919–21), all republicans fought together against the British; Ballylongford so prominently that part of it was burned by the Black and Tans. Then came the Treaty. The united republican movement divided into anti-Treaty ('republicans') and pro-Treaty ('free staters'). Literally (for instance in my own village) brother fought against brother. One thing that united people around here, healing the wounds of the Civil War, was football – the memories of the atrocities of the Civil War were put aside and free staters and republicans united on the playing field – the sight of John Joe Sheehy of Tralee (a republican) and Con Brosnan of Moyvane (a captain in the free state army) playing together on the county team in the 1920s and early 1930s was an example to all. The Kennellys were pro-Treaty, later Fine Gael. Ballylongford was, and is, strongly divided in its loyalties. When Kennelly supported Charles Haughey as a statesman and patron of the arts, his sister-in-law wrote to him enquiring 'What about the corkscrew?' Brendan, baffled, replied 'What corkscrew?' only to be reminded that his father used to opine that de Valera (founder of Fianna Fáil, Haughey's party) was so crooked that if he swallowed a nail, he'd shit a corkscrew! But Kennelly is a winger – he follows his own lights, playing the ball as it comes to him.

*

Religion is central to the life of rural Ireland. I say this in the full knowledge that religion plays a part in the lives of urban dwellers too. But it's different in the country. Everyone knows what everyone else is doing – there's not much hidden in a small village. Ballylongford, the 'Crooked Cross' of Kennelly's first novel (and the Kennellys lived at the intersection of that cross) is no different. The school system worked hand in hand with the Roman Catholic Church – faith was taught as if knowledge was belief. Pupils in Kennelly's day had their heads full of the big (theological) words which he has written about in his poem

'The Big Words': words that would protect against the 'evil',
'Godlessness' and 'worldliness' of England, in particular, and
the United States of America – Ireland was educating its youth
for emigration. The word that would protect, the sanctuary of
the word, the sacredness of the word. Kennelly learned the big
words, learned them very well. When he began to question
them, they yielded up a necessary alternative theology. The case
of Francis Xavier Skinner, in his poem 'The Sin', is instructive.
Skinner (Kennelly?) realises that sin flatters his own vanity, that
in reality he is only a puny little human trying to measure up to
God in the belief that his sin is important, original, and hurtful
to God. It is, of course, no such thing. It is an insult to love, no
more and no less. Later Skinner, having prayed to his maker 'To
give (him) the vision/To commit a significant sin', will become
Judas and the nightmare begins. I mentioned to Kennelly after
I had read *The Book of Judas* that I had profound difficulties
with the book, with the spirit of the book. When asked by him
for an instance, I mentioned what I felt to be the naked hatred
of women I had picked up here and there in the book. I had
no problem with the straightforwardness of *Cromwell*, where
Kennelly writes:

Drag the rat out here into the square.
Does he think he can write a book like this
And get away with it?
Christ Almighty, is there anything he won't say?
How can we protect ourselves against him?

But I found *Judas* offensive. Kennelly replied: 'Is it because you
think I hate women? I hate myself.' I believe that Kennelly's
sensibility is a fairly traditional Catholic one, part of which is
obsessed with sin and guilt. The poet John Berryman, likewise

afflicted, once told a story of a girl whose sense of sin he envied – she said prayers of thanksgiving after making love; Berryman could only feel guilt. The misplaced sense of sin is manifestly destructive. But Catholicism isn't entirely about sin – the true purpose of the confessional is to get rid of sin. The downside of confession is not an orthodox spiritual tyranny but the absolution from responsibility some expect from 'confessors/ Who would forgive [them] anything' as John Liddy has pointed out in his poem 'Southern Comfort'.

*

But the central problem for Kennelly is not sin nor Cromwell nor Judas. It is the problem of language, how to say himself. 'In the beginning was the Word', Kennelly often quotes, for, like many poets, he is obsessed with words. He wrote some years ago that it is as important to know where the words in your mouth come from as to know where the food in your mouth comes from. The word, the *logos,* is an abstract, intellectual concept, the mouth is not: it is physical, passionate, primal; with it we eat, we speak, we kiss. To Kennelly, words are physical. Irish, not long before Kennelly's birth, had been the first language of north Kerry (the census of 1901 shows that in Moyvane, neighbouring Ballylongford, there were still a few native Irish speakers). The Irish language went into decline mainly for economic reasons which, allied to a failure of nerve, a lack of confidence in the native language (the fact that it would be unable to translate itself on the streets of London or Liverpool, New York or New Orleans), was the death knell of spoken Irish throughout Ireland, except in the *Gaeltachtaí* where Irish remained the spoken language of the people.

But a language, in a sense, never dies. Though Kennelly's Buffún moans (in *Cromwell*):

I had a language once.
I was at home there.
Someone murdered it
Buried it somewhere.
I use different words now
Without skill, truly as I can.
A man without a language
Is half a man, if he's lucky

… he does not …

believe this language is dead.
Not a thousand years of hate could kill it,
Or worse, a thousand years of indifference.
So long as I live my language will live
Because it is mine …
Someone, somewhere, will learn.

Seán Ó Ríordáin (1917–77), the Irish language poet, wrote of
the echo that is heard even in places that have abandoned the
native dialect (in his poem 'Ceol Ceantair' [Local Music]). This
is true of villages like Ballylongford and the other north Kerry
villages. The language of the people was not Irish, it was not
English, it was not Hiberno-English. It was a language whose
accent, vocabulary and syntax were a translation from the Irish.
Words were taken from the Irish and 'Englished' – for instance
'kippen' from *cipín*, a twig, a little stick. Someone would ask you
to go out and bring in 'a *gwall* of kippens' – a *gabháil* (armful)
of twigs. Inevitably, some things had names then which have no
names now. I think of the word *scrá* (nearest English equivalent,
a clod). Boys would throw 'scraws' at each other for fun. They
still do occasionally, but now they have no name for what they

are throwing. Kennelly learned standard Hiberno-English in Ballylongford national school (where one of his teachers was Johnny Walsh, the great Kerry footballer) and later at Saint Ita's secondary school in Tarbert. Saint Ita's, and its founder and guiding spirit, the teacher Miss Jane Agnes McKenna, must be considered the significant event of Kennelly's early education. Jane Agnes McKenna was an enlightened teacher, strict but enabling, who recognised the potential of the young Kennelly. She facilitated him in every way and became, I suspect, the role model for Kennelly the teacher. In Saint Ita's, Kennelly encountered French and Latin, the one a modern language, the other providing him with the etymology he so desperately needed – and which informs him to this day.

Kennelly was a good student and was awarded a sizarship to Trinity College, Dublin, but because of shyness and a lack of confidence in himself, he left. He worked at various jobs – in the pub in Ballylongford, in the Electricity Supply Board, as a bus conductor in England, before re-entering Trinity, from which he graduated in 1961. In 1963 he was appointed to the Department of English there, was made a fellow in 1967, associate professor in 1969 and was appointed to the newly created chair of Modern Literature in 1973. English, Irish, his local dialect, French and Latin – words to discover, to savour, to create. This is Kennelly the communicator who insists that what he says (and writes) is well said, memorable, catchy. A deeper voice insists that it is profound, spiritual, searching. These tributaries converge in the ballad/lyric of his 'mainstream' poems.

*

The ballad is vital to the life of north Kerry. No team wins a football final that is not sung. Everything was celebrated in balladry here in Kennelly's youth – love lost and found, martyrdom (the martyrs of the War of Independence and Civil

War), sport (football and greyhounds mainly), emigration … The poet 'made' a ballad – 'writing' or 'composing' were not the terms. He (or she) made the ballad, and all the ballads had mythical qualities, for the men in them were not mere men but heroes, larger than life, the only limits on them what one could entertain. The ballad bound the tribe together. This is where Kennelly comes from – he is a ballad-maker, first and last. He extends the ballad by coupling it with the lyric, and the love child is born in the ear, sings in the ear, and is translated by the ear. This is the territory of passion, of the heart, of the force of personality where *how* a thing is said (rhythmically, rhetorically, dramatically, even melodramatically, but above all musically) is as important as what is said. To reduce it is to kill it. Kennelly's poetry is like a ritual: it involves more than the mind, more than the intellect, as a ballad insinuates itself with its music and hyperbole into an area of consciousness that is not appreciated by the reductive mind.

But let us not forget Moloney, a character as devious and cunning as Buffún, but, unlike Buffún, a hero. Indeed, Kennelly chastised me when I identified him with Buffún in my review of *Cromwell* in the *Kerryman* newspaper in December 1983, but blithely signed my copy of *Moloney Up and At It* as 'Moloney'. Who is Moloney? Judas is Moloney gone wrong. Moloney is the life force who witnesses the resurrection (of Kate Finucane), who makes love on his mother's grave, who receives the dust of the cremated Mike Nelligan courtesy of a 'tricky hoor of a Shannon wind', who in doing so takes death into himself and possesses it. If he will not, ultimately, triumph over death, he uses his wits to cheat it, to come to terms with it, to possess it. Death and life are one in Moloney. Moloney knows the place of sin in his life – that's his salvation; Judas doesn't and is damned. Moloney is, in many ways, the archetypal Kerryman – worldly-wise, cute (i.e. cunning), fun-loving, anecdotal, with flashes of the profound and otherworldly, but above all he doesn't take life (or sin) too seriously. He is rooted in himself and in his place.

Kennelly is rooted in two places – Ballylongford and Dublin. At home in both, they are, for him, places of permanent beginning, places of revelation. There is a sense that Kennelly exists in language – that without words there is no Kennelly. All his translation is a translation of Ballylongford. Time and again he returns to the happenings of his youth. His *Antigone, Medea, The Trojan Women* and *Blood Wedding* have their roots in the Ballylongford of his youth. He lives, for instance, with the memory of the local woman who railed at her dead husband to get up out of his coffin because his death betrayed her. There is too, as Peter Levi has pointed out (in 'The Lamentation of the Dead'), a Greek dimension to 'Caoineadh Airt Uí Laoghaire' (the 'Cry for Art O'Leary' so lovingly translated by Kennelly) – the keening of the dead unbroken from biblical times, from Homeric times right up to this lament for her dead husband by Eibhlín Dhubh Ní Chonaill in the late eighteenth century. 'With this poem,' Levi concludes, 'a world ended; we had not known that it had lived so long.' Its vestiges were to be found, until quite recently, in places like Ballylongford. What Kennelly translates is experience, the feel of a thing. He translates the spirit of a poem or play; he is no slave of the literal. Yet this approach is faithful and powerful as mere imitation is not – to render a poem or play word by word is to lose sight of the whole. Poetry is made in the translation, too. He can, on occasion, remain quite close to the text – as he often does in the shorter Irish lyrics which he has published in *A Drinking Cup* and *Love of Ireland* which are faithfully translated in sound and sense.

Seán Ó Ríordáin wrote that poetry was to be *fé ghné eile*

(under another aspect, to enter the other). Translation is for Kennelly one such vehicle. But then Cromwell and Judas are translations too. Becoming the other, giving voice to the other … For, like all poets, Kennelly is both himself and other. He once wrote to me that 'There's nothing musical that isn't a deepdown war'. It started, perhaps, with his 'Blackbird':

> I scarce believe his murderous competence
> As he stabs to stay alive,
> Choking music
> That music may survive

and continued in the other ballad/lyrics where the objective world of the ballad enters the subjective world of the lyric; it was furthered in translation – entering the other. But there is, for him, an end to that road. It is, then, no wonder that he eventually exploded into the epic mode. Some things are too big for ballads and lyrics. They must be all-inclusive, they must howl and sprawl. Kennelly's epics translate him into the other. Kennelly, like all poets (and wingers!) writes his own rules – at its greatest this is a revelation, at its least it's merely 'to shake the hoors up' as he has said to me more than once. Like his second cousin, Robert Leslie Boland (1888–1955), 'The Poet-Farmer of Faranastack' whose poems were published in book form for the first time in 1993, he can be sublime or vulgar, but never ridiculous. He carries Ballylongford, his crooked cross, with him as he carries his alter egos, his deities and his demons, his passions and his depressions, his alcoholism. The demons he sees in his loved ones terrify him, the demons in himself do not. He confronts his obsessions aggressively, even violently, as a man goes for the ball; he can also, like a good footballer, create his own space as he goes for the goal. Tender and violent, loving

and fearful, a rooted man, he has absorbed his childhood and
early years. The boy who saw

    … the darkness and the shame
    That could compel a man to turn his face
    Against the wall, withdrawn from light so strong
    And undeceiving, spancelled in a place
    Of unapplauding hands and broken song

now says it all and hides nothing. He exists in language. He is
because he says. He is what he says.

33

From Pig-Killer to Rain-Man: Brendan Kennelly's *The Man Made of Rain*

We should be grateful for Brendan Kennelly – for a man who lives his life in public, who has turned the private lyric into the public poem. 'Try not to lie', he exhorts himself in his book-length poem, *The Man Made of Rain*. Kennelly's is a search for truth – not a philosophical truth, but a poetic one; a truth, perhaps which, like Patrick Kavanagh's, flies 'beyond the proveable'.

For Kennelly, poetry is a gift – it 'took me unawares/And I accepted it' he informs us in an early lyric. His journey through life has been a poetic pilgrimage. His early poetry was lyrical, singing, meditative, insightful – in a word, beautiful. But as Kennelly descended into hell, as each poet must at some stage or another, all changed, changed utterly. The lyric no longer served him. He had to sprawl and fall in poetry; he had to say it all. And so he gave us three epic poems. ('An epic', he now asserts, 'is one word explored …/Until it's glad to surrender/ [its] secrets'). Thus, his *Cromwell* confronted the nightmare of history; *The Book of Judas* spent a season in hell; and *Poetry My Arse* looked into the void. There, he questioned everything – even poetry, his very *raison d'être*. The man made of rain goes beyond. Beyond nightmare, beyond history, beyond hell, beyond the void. In this poem, written while Kennelly was recovering from quadruple bypass surgery, he tells us of the visions he had when he was between life and death the day after the operation. In them, he sees a man made of rain who speaks to him and takes him on journeys to places such as his father's grave, inside his father's bones, the land of no-language, the place where scars are roads through difficult territories, provinces of history and memory. The man made of rain brings him to moments of definition, to a 'dreamsurrender' that is 'articulate and vital'. So nightmare becomes vision. A transformation takes place. All through this poem, there is this kind of transformation and, therefore, healing. As Kennelly's heart heals so does his life.

What is the man made of rain? Rain has long been a symbol of fertility, of growth, of rebirth among so called 'primitive' or 'aboriginal' cultures. Theirs is a dream culture, a culture of healing visions. The male rain fertilises the female soil causing the crops to grow, the rivers to flow, resurrecting nature, replenishing life. But what is Kennelly's rain-man? He, too, is a symbol of fertility: he is 'the heaven's own rain'. He, too, is a bringer of life – the life, among other things, of the word. 'There'd be a noticeable decline in life-giving talk if heaven sent us less rain', Kennelly writes. And, echoing the Hail Mary, he salutes the rain – 'Hail, full of stories' he exclaims. The healing is a spiritual as well as a physical one – the heart is, after all, not only the iambic pulse of our lives, but the seat of all our feelings.

In an early poem, the young Kennelly describes a pig-killer:

… Tenderly his fingers move
On the flabby neck, seeking the right spot
For the knife. Finding it, he leans
Nearer and nearer the waiting throat,

Expert fingers fondling flesh. Nodding then
To Gorman and Dineen, he raises the knife,

Begins to trace a line along the throat.
Slowly the line turns red, the first sign

Of blood appears, spreads shyly over the skin.

Note the gentleness of the words. The pig-killer fingers the pig *tenderly*, he *fondles* the pig's flesh. The blood appears *slowly*, *shyly*. Now look at his transformation in *The Man Made of Rain*. Kennelly writes:

I see the wounded sky ...

> and though the sky is bleeding
> the wound, slowly and shyly,
> begins to sing.

The wound that killed the pig heals Kennelly. Saint John of the Cross, in his *Dark Night of the Soul*, speaks of the gentle wound that causes all his senses to be suspended so that he can abandon himself, leaving his cares forgotten among the lilies. And in another poem of his, 'Living Flame of Love', he speaks of the delectable wound that savours of eternal life, that, in slaying the 'old man', the world that is too much with us, makes way for the new life of the spirit, and thus changes death into life. This is what Kennelly is doing here: he is changing death into life – through him, with him, in him. 'The wound of love's the most living thing', he discovers because 'Love shines through death' and 'Death disappears/in the eyes of rain'. Kennelly has taken on death and renews himself, revives himself. 'Is there anything more sweet and sane/than to lie/between living and dying/and listen to the rain?' he sings. For Kennelly has learned to abandon himself: he will let whatever happens happen to him, he tells us.

To let whatever happens happen. To go beyond fear, beyond hell, beyond life and death. Beyond … What is beyond? Nothing. 'Think', he writes, 'of the beauty of nothing'. 'What is flesh? …/A kind of everything waiting to be nothing', he learns. Nothing. No-thing. A no-thing has no boundaries, no limits, is not finite. He is no longer bound by being a thing – he is content 'to drift …without a care,/in or out of the world' in 'a land of no-language …/before the first word is born' where 'happiness is possible' and 'peace is happy to live'.

'All the gods are happy to smile/but men of flesh won't let them', he admonishes us. Kennelly is happy to let the gods smile. And they do. Kennelly is at peace now, and can smile with the gods, for, like Robert Browning, Kennelly's 'God [is] in heaven' and the 'years are turning fresh again'. 'The heart is fun', he recognises, and 'something is having mercy/on [him]'. He thanks 'the heart of sickness/for the man of rain', his salvation.

Kennelly is transformed in this book – from pig-killer to healer, from death to life, from fear to song, from hell to heaven. In doing so, he shows us a way, a truth, a life:

Between the idea
And the reality …
Falls the Shadow

… the poet Eliot tells us in a world of hollow men. Kennelly knows better. He has found that (to parody Eliot):

Between the dream
And the waking
Falls the rain.

34

'[An] Exile out Foreign in 'Glantine':
Michael Hartnett and the Sense of Place

I first met Michael Hartnett in 1979. I had recently joined Writers' Week, the literary festival in Listowel, and was director of its newly composed ballad competition. I travelled to Michael's house in Templeglantine to invite him to adjudicate the competition. He, a ballad lover himself, readily agreed. On the night of the competition, Michael, just to prove his credentials as a ballad-maker, sang his 'The Ballad of the Books', the chorus of which goes:

> Well you're not the *Kama Sutra*
> And you're not *Ulysses*,
> *The Guinness Book of Records*,
> *The Old Man and the Seas* [*sic.*],
> *The Origin of Species*,
> *The Voyage of Captain Cook*,
> I know everything about you,
> I can read you like a book.

Michael and I quickly became friends. We would meet every week in Newcastle West, drink pints of Guinness and talk in Irish or English as the humour took us. The talk was mostly about poetry – what he was writing, what I was trying to write. He encouraged me greatly. Though he was ruthless with a red biro, crossing out words, lines and stanzas of my fledgeling poems (and sometimes even the entire poems!) he persevered with me. I remember one night in the Devon Inn in Templeglantine; our talk, as usual, was of poetry. Suddenly Michael demanded '*An file tusa?*' ('Are you a poet?'). He knew that I would feel too shy and unworthy to answer 'yes'. When I demurred, he persisted, asking again and again '*An file tusa?*' till in desperation I exploded: 'Oh, to hell with it, *is file mé*' ('I am a poet').

Michael was best man at our wedding in 1981. Brenda, my wife and I, would often visit the Hartnetts in Templeglantine where Michael, *Larousse Gastronomique* to hand, would cook the most sumptuous meals. Those were the good days in the Hartnett household. Later, things would change.

Michael had returned at the onset of middle age to Newcastle West to write poetry. He also involved himself with the local arts scene, bringing, among others, Seamus Heaney and the Australian poet, Vincent Buckley, to read in Newcastle West. Let Vincent Buckley, from his memoir 'Memory Ireland', take up the tale:

As we [i.e. Hartnett and himself] walked to the hotel where we were to attend some meeting, he said, 'Don't say anything against Heaney in this town.' 'I wouldn't dream of it,' I said. 'Why do you mention it?' It appeared that, some months earlier, Heaney had given a reading there, and had then stayed at the bar until very late drinking with his local admirers and other clean-minded types. Among these was the town bore who, as the night wore on, annexed Heaney more and more. Heaney coped courteously with all this, but the speaker was so boring that the other drinkers moved slowly away from him. At last, in the middle of a sentence, the poor bore collapsed, and slid slowly down the bar to lie at Heaney's feet. He, looking around, called to the nearest deserter,

'Would you mind giving me a hand?' and, with the volunteer thus chosen by the Chinese system, carried the man over and laid him carefully on a couch. 'They've never stopped talking about it,' said Hartnett. 'Heaney's king around here.'

Buckley also describes the night of his own reading in Newcastle West. He was to have read, with me in support, in the Desmond Banqueting Hall. On the appointed night, nobody turned up for the reading. '[T]here were doors to be opened, lights to be turned up, a hundred chairs to be brought and set up,' Buckley informs us. (What had happened was that Michael had mistakenly advertised the reading for the following night). There was nothing for it but to adjourn to Eddie Lynch's Bar where Buckley and my wife and I fell into conversation. One of the invited musicians arrived in the bar but, try as I would, I couldn't persuade him to play. Eventually Gerry Murphy, the banjo player, and Donie Nolan, the accordion player, happened upon us and they, in the full flower of youth, were game for a session. So Gerry and Donie played and I joined them on my guitar. Meanwhile Michael, worried that Buckley would have no fee for the 'reading', set off on a tour of the local public houses, collecting what he could from the locals. He arrived in Lynch's some time later with a fistful of pound notes which he duly gave to Buckley. Honour was satisfied.

Michael will be remembered as a gifted lyric poet who drew together the two linguistic strands of our country. In English and Irish he left a corpus of work, the best of which will be appreciated as long as poetry is read.

I want to look at two of Michael Hartnett's poems which I consider to be crucial to Hartnett the poet and the man. The two poems are 'Maiden Street Ballad' and 'Inchicore Haiku'.

Michael Hartnett was a voluntary exile. Unlike Joyce and

the rest he didn't need to flee Ireland to be an exile. He was an internal exile, exiling himself from the things, and even the people, he loved.

The title of this essay is taken from 'Maiden Street Ballad', his lighthearted homage to his native Newcastle West. In it, he describes himself as being 'in exile out foreign in 'Glantine', that is in Templeglantine, just outside Newcastle West, where he lived in the townland of Glendarragh until he further exiled himself to Dublin, c. 1985. The period is roughly between the publication in 1975 of his *A Farewell to English* and his *Inchicore Haiku*, the book that marked his return to that language, in 1985.

In describing himself as an 'exile out foreign in 'Glantine' he deliberately echoes Aindrias Mac Craith (1710–95) who was known as 'An Mangaire Súgach' ('The Merry Pedlar'). Mac Craith was a hero of Hartnett's, being singled out for mention in *A Farewell to English* along with his other heroes, the dispossessed Gaelic poets Dáibhí Ó Bruadair (c. 1625–98) and Aogán Ó Rathaille (c. 1675–1729). Mac Craith was denounced by the parish priest of Croom for his dissolute life which he, Mac Craith, interpreted as a banishment. In consequence, he took himself off to the parish of Ballyneety, some ten miles from Croom, where the priest, being himself a poet, was more liberal and charitable to Mac Craith's amorous and alcoholic proclivities. In exile, and in dejection, Mac Craith composed 'Slán le Máigh', one of our finest songs of exile in Irish or English which begins

Slán is céad ón taobh so uaim
Cois Mháighe na gcaor na gcraobh na gcruach
Na stát na séad na saor na slua
Na ndán na ndréacht na dtréan gan ghruaim.

Och, ochón, is breoite mise,
Gan chuid gan chóir gan chóip gan chiste
Gan sult gan seoid gan spórt gan spionnadh
Ó seoladh mé chun uaignis.

(A fond farewell I send from here
To Maigue's fair fields where produce teems,
That peopled, pearled, plenteous scene
Of tales and tunes and hearts' good cheer.

Alas! my woe, my low condition,
No food, no friends, no rights, no riches,
No joy, no jewels, no sport, no spirit,
Now doomed to dwell an outcast.)

– translated by Criostoir O'Flynn

Hartnett is an exile not even ten miles from his native Newcastle West! Up to then he had lived for periods in England, in Spain (from where he was deported with his passport confiscated by Franco's regime), and in Dublin. In 1975, with the publication of *A Farewell to English*, he signalled his intention to exile himself from the English language and to write in Irish only. With this in mind, he returned to west Limerick, to Templeglantine, which he considered to be a *breac Ghaeltacht*, a place where Irish, though not universally spoken, was widely understood. In Templeglantine with Rosemary, his English wife (who hadn't a word of Irish), and children Lara and Niall, he settled down to write in Irish. He published *Adharca Broic* in 1978, *An Phurgóid* in 1983, *do Nuala: Foidhne Chrainn* in 1984 and *An Lia Nocht* in 1985. This was the work he released to the general public.

But in the background he was writing ballads in English, some of them, under the *nom de plume* 'The Wasp', scurrilous excoriations of perceived meanness in Newcastle West. In 'Maiden Street Ballad' he cites the example of Aherne and Barry, both local poets, before him:

So come all you employers, beware how you act
for a poet is never afraid of a fact:
your grasping and greed I will always attack
like Aherne and Barry before me.
My targets are only the mean and the proud
and the vandals who try to make dirt of this town,
if their fathers were policemen they'd still feel the clout
of public exposure in poetry.

'Maiden Street Ballad' is unquestionably the best ballad he wrote during this period. It is a celebration of his native place in which he describes mainly the period 1948–51, the time of his childhood; it also describes the Newcastle West of the late 1970s during which time he lived in Templeglantine.

In the early part of the poem he speaks of the poverty of his childhood years:

Now before you get settled, take a warning from me
for I'll tell you some things that you won't like to hear –
we were hungry and poor down in Lower Maiden Street,
a fact I will swear on the Bible.
There were shopkeepers then, quite safe and secure –
seven masses a week and then shit on the poor:
ye know who I mean, of that I am sure,
and if they like, they can sue me for libel.

But though they were poor, and emigration was taking its toll, the children were not unhappy there, playing games like pitch-and-toss and marbles, 'rawking' (i.e. robbing) orchards, swapping comics, catching 'collies' (minnows) in jam jars and hunting for 'craw-fish' (cray fish).

He describes the exodus in 1951 from their homes in Maiden Street up the hill to Assumpta Park, the new local authority housing scheme:

> The old street it finally gave up the ghost,
> and most of the homes there they got the death-blow
> when most of the people were tempted to go
> and move to the Hill's brand-new houses.
> The moving it started quite soon after dark
> and the handcars and wheelbars pushed off to the Park
> and some of the asscars were like Noah's Ark
>   with livestock and children and spouses.
>
> For we took all our furniture there when we moved,
> our flourbags and teachests and three legged stools
> and stowaway mice ahide in old boots
>   and jamcrocks in good working order.
> And our fleas followed after – our own local strain –
> they said 'We'll stand by ye whatever the pain,
> for our fathers drew life from yere fathers' veins
>   and blood it is thicker than water'! …
>
> In nineteen-fifty-one people weren't too smart:
> in spite of the toilets they pissed out the back,
> washed feet in the lavatry, put coal in the bath
>   and kept the odd pig in the garden.
> They burnt the bannisters for to make fires
> and pumped up the Primus for the kettle to boil,
> turned on all the taps, left the lights on all night –
>   but these antics I'm sure you will pardon.

For in a few years we all settled down
and quickly became the pride of the town –
we swapped our old army coats for eiderdowns
        and stopped being so wild and so airy.
We have motorcars now and we sometimes play squash,
and dirty or clean, quite often we wash:
we have more than one shirt and more than two socks
        and we holiday in the Canaries.

He describes his love of his native place:

But what can I say of a small country town
that is not like Killarney, known all the world round?
That has not for beauty won fame or renown
        but still all the same is quite charming?
I have seen some fine cities in my traveller's quest,
put Boston and London and Rome to the test
but I wouldn't give one foot of Newcastle West
        for all of their beauty and glamour.

Go out some fine evening, walk up to the Park
when the sun shines on Rooska and the Galtees are dark
and all the nice gardens are tidy and smart
        and the dogs lie asleep in the roadway:
and the blue of the hills with their plumes of white smoke
in a hazy half-circle do shelter our homes
and the crows to the treetops fly home in black rows
        and the women wheel out their new go-cars.

When the children in dozens are playing at ball
and Dick Fitz and Mike Harte stand and chat by the wall
and a hundred black mongrels do bark and do brawl
        and scratch their backsides in the street there:

174

when the smell of black pudding it sweetens the air
and the scent of back rashers it spreads everywhere
and the smoke from the chimneys goes fragrant and straight
    to the sky in the Park in the evening.

These verses are balladry at its best. They are passionate and direct, catchy and memorable like their famous model, the song 'The Limerick Rake' which Hartnett described as 'the best Hiberno-English ballad ever written in this county'. Hartnett's ballad was written, he tells us in the preface, 'not with mockery but with affection – part funny song, part social history. Ballads about places however bad they may be, unite a community and give it a sense of identity.' He completed 'Maiden Street Ballad' in December 1980.

But things were going wrong for him in his beloved west Limerick: he was drinking heavily, his marriage was breaking down and, on 3 October 1984, his father died.

Again, Hartnett goes into exile – away from his wife and family, away from Newcastle West. He sets off for Dublin. This will mark his return to the English language, though he will continue to write in Irish also.

Again he is challenged by his sense of place. Shortly after his arrival in Dublin he publishes his *Inchicore Haiku*, a homage to Inchicore, his new place, a sequence of eighty-seven haiku in English, all in the traditional seventeen syllables. He begins (in Haiku 8) with

My English dam bursts
and out stroll my bastards.
Irish shakes its head.

Later, he concludes that:

Banished for treason,
for betraying my country.
I live in myself.

Alone in Dublin, living in himself (as a poet must), he admits that he is drinking himself to death:

My liver sneers up
from the bottom of a glass
snug in golden hell.

He misses the country:

I want the country:
here trees grow out of cement.
And paper leaves fall.

Still, *in extremis*, he tells us:

I make my sad verse
but hope keeps interfering
forget-me-nots wink.

He is in his final exile. Away from home, away from his family and his people in west Limerick, his plight is not unlike that of the seventeenth and eighteenth-century Gaelic poets he so admires who are exiled from their culture and are destitute. But though they are destitute, hope, for them too, keeps interfering: in their *aisling* poems, they express the hope that a redeemer will come to rescue them.

Hartnett tells us that he is dying. Though he doesn't actually die until 1999, he knows that this is the end game. He tells us (in haiku 82) that:

Dying in exile.
To die without a people
is the real death.

But again hope interferes. Though he is in exile, he is not without a people. In Inchicore, he finds a people, a working class people that he, like his father before him, a house painter and Labour Party supporter, can identify with, to whom he can belong:

All divided up,
all taught to hate each other.
Are these my people?

My dead father shouts
from his eternal Labour:
'These are your people!'

In Templeglantine and in Inchicore, both places of exile, Hartnett the poet can find a people. Though a perpetual exile, an internal exile, nevertheless he can take a place into himself and celebrate it. In *Maiden Street Ballad* and *Inchicore Haiku*, Michael Hartnett demonstrates that the ballad and the haiku, like the *aisling* poems of old, can indeed bond a community together, and though the poet must necessarily be an outsider, he too can inhabit that community.

35

A Stoic's World: Dennis O'Driscoll's *Exemplary Damages*

Dennis O'Driscoll is one of the reasons we can continue to believe in contemporary poetry. His lucid, uncompromising, profound yet playful intelligence looks into the heart of darkness and returns to tell its tale. He is unflinchingly honest where a lesser poet would settle for the softer option, the easy resolution.

The poems in his collection *Exemplary Damages* visit familiar O'Driscoll territory – love, death, work. As I read him, he seems to be saying that there is an inevitability about life that is alleviated, if not quite redeemed, by literature (including, I believe, scripture) and art.

In O'Driscoll's world, to work is to pray even if it is prayer in the secular sense: work brings its own consolations, the satisfaction of a job well done is its own reward. Consider the 'Technicians, overseers, assistant/depot managers, stock controllers./Old fashioned nine-to-five men' in their 'diamond-patterned sweaters' who, unknown to their calorie-counting wives, tuck into a fry on pay day. They might be Eliot's hollow men but not in O'Driscoll's view. Their lives might have drifted some distance from the passion of primary meaningfulness, but O'Driscoll informs us that 'there are worse fates' and that 'they know [it] well enough'. These people are content with their lot, they are not consumed by worldly ambition. Their reward is that 'Life tastes great some days'.

To the casual eye, this world might seem jaded; in a world where 'Our one true God has died' living might seem pointless. This is a world that, in the name of human kindness, remains 'eternally precious in the eyes of man', a world where 'We love one another so much the slightest/hurt cries out for compensation: sprain your/ankle in a pothole and City Hall will pay/exemplary damages for your pains'; a world where 'we are equal under the law as we once were/in [God's] sight'; a world where just as once we were all accounted for by a loving God, we are now 'enshrined in police department databases,/our good names maintained by the recording/angels of mailshot sales campaigns,/rewarded with chainstore loyalty points'.

This is a world where God has given way to Mammon. And yet in the third section of the title poem, 'Exemplary Damages', O'Driscoll writes: 'The baby is at the end/of its umbilical tether, awaiting delivery…/The doctor is alert…/The father has brought/a cellophane-sheathed baby seat/for installation in the family car./The mother is ready/to stifle cries of distress/at the wellhead of her breast./Wool blankets to hand,/they are all on standby/like a search and rescue party/keeping vigil near a cave'. If there are no angels in the sky announcing the birth of a saviour, that cave still betokens a Christmas and there's a search and rescue party keeping vigil near the child.

This book is full of such moments. 'How fresh this stale world seems' O'Driscoll exults. (This from a person whose 'sentence [of death by illness] is deferred'.) Though he knows that the sentence is merely deferred, nonetheless he can exult: he knows he is racing towards infinity. Even when, in another poem, a mother (at least, this is how I read it) dies, the children manage fine, make break-fasts and make love, take on jobs and mortgages, set themselves up for life. 'And yet. And yet. And yet' O'Driscoll concludes this poem. Regret, like the poor, we have always with us.

We might even be tempted to 'call it a day, abandon/the entire perverted experiment [of life]'. We might be disinclined to 'bestir ourselves to purge/the unholy mess'. Even if 'It was all destined to end badly.../at the city dump/where fridges pour out their gasesous souls/and black plastic sacks spill synthetic/viscera for pillaging shanty dwellers/to scavenge, reap what we have sown', life still goes on, a more vital life scavenges the cast-offs of a jaded society. Even *in extremis,* there is, if not quite a reason to hope, then a reason to live. At the very least, there is no reason for dejection.

The crucial question is the existence or non existence of God. '[T]hough we rebelled against Him/... we confess to missing Him at times./Miss Him during the civil wedding/... [waiting] in vain/to be fed a line containing words/like "everlasting" and "divine".../Miss Him when we stumble on the breast lump/for the first time and an involuntary prayer/escapes our lips.../Miss Him when we call out His name/spontaneously in awe or anger/as a woman in a birth ward bawls/her long-dead mother's name'. God is dead. So far, so good. But though He may be dead, we can't help resurrecting His memory in art, in literature, in the ordinariness of our lives. We miss Him, O'Driscoll writes, 'when the linen-covered/dining table holds warm bread-rolls,/shiny glasses of red wine'. The God of our imagination lives. Thus the artist Osias Beert, painting a bowl of fresh cherries, can 'set aside/his griefs to let joy have its way'. He is 'satisfied with his lot/even if the rot will set in soon/and the freshness is pure deception/lasting no longer than cherry blossoms/tossed on snow when north winds/are enjoying their final fling'. There are times, his painting seems to say 'when, despite all/evidence to the contrary, life is/... a bowl of cherries'. And though the painter may be 'far off/the mark where truth (whatever/about beauty) is concerned,/the cherries – bite-size apples –/tempt with their own improbable/knowledge and the cold viewer's/eyes helplessly assent'.

One of the words that best sums up O'Driscoll's world is that word 'despite'. He seems to be saying, if I read him correctly, that despite everything life still goes on. He can still credit marvels, the little miracles and epiphanies that rise out of our daily lives. The Romantic spirit, like 'Romantic England', despite its many faults 'is neither dead nor gone'. He can take time to stand and stare and listen to a thrush in expiring light as the day slips 'through the gnarly fingers of old trees;/a music inducing the absurd spectacle/of a man (myself, say) looking to a bird,/of all things, in a digital epoch,/for entertainment, maybe even truth'. The light is expiring, it is the dying of the light, the self conscious intelligence, looking for entertainment, maybe even truth, listens to a thrush singing. One part, the twenty-first century logical part, of O'Driscoll knows that this is absurd. Like Osias Beert he 'may be far off/the mark where truth … is concerned' but the Romantic notion that beauty is truth, truth beauty is not entirely suspended. Faced by compelling beauty, he can but 'helplessly assent'.

In the end, however, he knows, like Philip Larkin, that he is 'going/to the inevitable' – death. Since his poem 'Someone', and others like it, appeared in his first collection, *Kist*, in 1982, O'Driscoll has been obsessed with death. He sees the skull beneath the skin. If at times he has come perilously close to being morbid, the older O'Driscoll can now observe death with a more playful eye. In 'Saturday Night Fever' (a deliciously punny title) he tells us that 'Playing tonight at the X-Ray-Ted Club,/[are] The Chemotherapies, drugged to the gills,/the lead singer's pate modishly bald/And who will your partner be?/Alzheimer, the absent-minded type,/with the retro gear, everything a perfect mismatch?/Huntington, grooving his hippy-hippy-shake routine?/

Thrombosis, the silly clot, trying to pull a stroke?' And so on.

It's not that he is trivialising death. He is still obsessed with it, only differently now. Older, and wiser, he can take a less sober, more upbeat (though still chilling), view of the inevitable. It would be easy for such a view to descend to a vision of the absurd. It would be easy for such a vision to pronounce that life is absurd. O'Driscoll does not. 'Wiping clean the day's dark slate', he concludes in the final poem, 'sleep sweeps you off your feet,/leaves you dead to the world/in your bedclothes, shrouded in sheets'. This is, I contend, a late Christian vision. I would hesitate to term it post Christian though I may be wrong.

In conclusion, O'Driscoll re-enacts a confession, the Christian sacrament of penance (or reconciliation as we view it in the light of today) – the day's dark slate is *'wiped clean';* 'sleep *sweeps you off your feet'* (there is something astonishing, something miraculous implied in the phrase), and it 'leaves you *dead to the world'.* The condition of being dead to the world is one that many mystics and holy men and women, Christian and non-Christian, have striven for throughout the ages: to be dead to the world is to be alive to the otherworld – however we may wish to name it. The day's slate wiped clean, swept off our feet, dead to the world, shrouded in sheets (like Christ in the tomb), though iffy about 'His Second Coming', we turn to the word, the imagination for expression.

Expression, it has been said, is the opposite of depression. It is not an entirely hopeless world. There are inevitabilities – birth, copulation and death. The search for consolation, for succour, might be an easier option but, for O'Driscoll, life goes on to its inevitable conclusion. Life goes on. And O'Driscoll in his poetry has achieved a reconciliation with life, an acceptance of the world as a valley of tears. This is essentially a Christian way of looking at the world and even if O'Driscoll doesn't make the necessary leap of faith that would redeem this 'unholy mess', it is nonetheless a world he is wholly committed to, a world that occupies and pre-occupies him wholly. It may be as much as one can hope for in the current milieu.

This is a book of such revelations, advancing the meaning of words (through their multi-layered richnesses) and, consequently, of meaning, to another plane. In a world that debases language (and to debase language is to debase life), where 'The word *forever* as used/in a pop song chorus./The word *vintage* as it occurs/in the second-hand shop-talk/of the clothes store – say, in/this label: *Vintage Slip, 1980s'* render the concepts of 'forever' and 'vintage' meaningless – the poet must revive the language so misused. This O'Driscoll does profoundly and playfully using the multiple meanings and nuances of words to enrich life in all its teeming multiplicity. Indeed, the entire book might be an attempt 'to revive/the life you lived once', a desire to return to the condition of Browning's certainty that 'God's in his heaven –/All's right with the world'. (And in passing, might I mention that, in contrast to Browning's use of the lower case 'his', O'Driscoll's constant use of the higher case 'His' when the pronoun refers to God is a touching, and revealing, reminder that, though God might be dead to the world, respect for the word, and consequently for God, or at the very least, the concept of God, is still a matter of concern to O'Driscoll). But O'Driscoll resists the temptation to dwell in the past. In his poetry he revives the life by reviving the word, but though he might hanker for the past, he doesn't dwell in it. His poetry is for today.

Exemplary Damages is a beautifully written account of a life that faces the modern dilemma of finding meaning in life where God is, at best, at a distance, and the traditional view of religion is of little help. O'Driscoll's is a stoic's world made bearable by the epiphanies of language and literature and art.

36

Irish Poetry Now: Other Voices

For too long there has been consensus about the state of Irish poetry. Hierarchies have been established, *saoithe* elevated to positions that are as meaningless as they are irrelevant. What does it mean to be a poet in Ireland as we approach the twenty-first century?

For me, poetry is about moments, insights. Poetry is all around us – it only remains for us to see it. Many see; the poet is the one who 'words' it. This is where much contemporary poetry has failed the educated reader: it is too selfish, too self indulgent, too obscure. Many poets are making themselves irrelevant.

A poet 'captures' nothing – he is not a policeman! He presents us with moments won from the daily drudge; he brings us moments which surprise us, for revelation is always new. There is poetry in the air around us, in the games we play, in the daily intercourse of our lives. Poetry is never precious; it is vital and enabling. It is that which most puts us in touch with ourselves, with our environment. It is that which is unique within us. It is that which is indomitable and, therefore, ever free. Creative or destructive, it takes us beyond ourselves, our limitations; ever restless, it seeks out new adventure. Poetry is a lonely occupation, an obsession born of inspiration. Poetry is inspired and it is inspiring. There are only two criteria with regard to poetry – that it has something to say, and that it is well said. The rest we can consign to the critics!

Certainly, there are many good poems (and poets) in the anthologies of the literary establishment. The purpose of the anthology, *Irish Poetry Now: Other Voices*, which I edited in 1994, was to show the breadth and depth of contemporary Irish poetry. There is an element of *uisce faoi thalamh*, a subterranean flow, about poetic endeavour that is often missed by the uninquisitive eye.

This, then is an anthology of Irish poetry conceived, translated into English, or published in the 1980s, a decade that saw much poetic activity on this island – a decade that saw the death of Liam Miller and his Dolmen Press; a decade that saw the growth of poetry presses – Raven, Beaver Row, Dedalus, Salmon, Cló Iar-Chonnachta and Coiscéim – which have published many valuable poets for the first time. I perceive my function as editor to be one of presenting a selection of the best verse available from the best poets available, to show the range of this poetry, and to introduce the reader to some new voices.

It is an anthology of *Irish* poetry. By *Irish poets* I mean poets born in Ireland, poets of Irish ancestry, and non-nationals who have been resident in Ireland for long periods, who have an interest in Ireland, and who have published in Ireland. Leopold Bloom stated that 'A nation is the same people living in the same place ... or also living in different places'. Patrick Galvin, living in a more consciously pluralist society, acknowledges the non-purity of nationality:

From these two I was born
The Ganges swaying with the Lee.

Nationality is a state of mind, an agreement. There is a citizenship of desire. The price of modern man's adaptability is his divided mind. This is the basis of his self criticism which, destructively, may sometimes lead to false assertions of national purity and, in extreme cases, to racism; creatively, it leads to art.

Much of this dividedness manifests itself in language – nowhere more so than in Ireland with its two languages, one tribal, ancestral, the other grafted to the old stock, both now part of the rose bush that is Ireland. Moya Cannon speaks of the racial memory that calls on the reserves of the native tongue where 'the word comes when needed'. These 'small unassailable words/that diminish caesars' are part of the latent vocabulary of many Irish people to this day – these words are:

> a testimony
> to waves succumbed to
> and survived.

The native tongue can be generous, too, to the innocence and ignorance of the monoglot English speaker who must translate the native in terms of the imported. Thus Art Ó Maolfabhail, in his poem 'Inis Córthaidh agus Gné den Stair', will freely pardon the girl who asked him what his name is in English. In the same vein, he writes of the 1798 rebellion:

> Ní mór peacaí ró-ghránna
> na staire a mhaitheamh.
> (We must pardon
> history's ugly sins.)

Coupled with this willingness to forgive and be forgiven is the desire for justice. Indeed, for many poets, the notion goes hand in hand with religion and spirituality. In his poem for Father Romano, Desmond Egan alludes to:

> the few
> who hand out like bread to others
> their ordinary life

Their lives are testimony that 'the resurrection continues' despite the tyrannies that attempt to:

> bundle truth into a jeep
> and stub out freedom with cigarette butts
> and build walls higher than the sky.

A welcome phenomenon of the 1980s was the coming to prominence of many gifted women poets. To this day, despite their emergence (from small presses, notably Salmon, Coiscéim and Beaver Row), they have received scant attention, critical or otherwise. Máire Bradshaw's *Box* (of poems) *Under the Bed* may be:

> a monument
> to burnt potatoes
> and overcooked
> beef

but it is also her 'emancipation'. I feel that the Irish language has had a greater welcome for its women than English. A poet like Máire Mhac an tSaoi has been influential since the 1950s when her first collection, *Margadh na Saoire*, was published. At this time, her sister poets in English were, mainly, condemned to silence by the other great censorship of the time – the censorship of women and womanhood.

In its censorship of literature and women, Ireland was manifesting a narrowness, a single-mindedness inimical to the maturity appropriate to a *free state*. In the new state that the gombeens, as Michael D. Higgins reminds us, decided 'Was a good thing/Even for business', an alternative to the official view, the party line, was, at best, suspicious. The divided mind, that nagging in the conscience that was necessary for the liberation of women (and writers) was, seemingly, anathema to the patriarchs of the time. It has taken until now for Ireland to utter, in the words of Brian Friel's Hugh in *Translations*, that 'confusion is not an ignoble condition'. In achieving their freedom of utterance, their emancipation, poets like Moya Cannon, Joan McBreen, Rita Ann Higgins, Caitlín Maude, Áine Ní Ghlinn, Mary O'Donnell and others not only articulate an area of consciousness, of humanity hitherto unavailable from most poetry presses, they strike a blow for the liberation of consciousness in general.

Many of the poems are concerned with death – the death of family, of language, of traditions, of love. Dermot Bolger's *Lament for Arthur Cleary*, more than most, I feel, encapsulates the great loss of death. Using an eighteenth century Irish lament (Eibhlín Dhubh Ní Chonaill's 'Caoineadh Airt Uí Laoghaire') as a model, he translates modern Irish urban experience – drug abuse, money lending, crime – with one eye on the older, rural, Gaelic tradition. Here is a true meeting of traditions, languages, cultures and literatures. If the poem ends with the death of Arthur Cleary, nonetheless his survivor, his lover

… will breathe [his] name
On the lips of another's children

Like a secretive tongue
They will carry in their hearts
To the foreign factories
In which their lives will pass.

Translated into European terms, and how appropriate it is that Tomás Mac Síomóin, writing in Irish, admits a European dimension here, the fate of Paul Celan serves as a reminder that death shall have no dominion, the grave no victory:

> … féach, a Celan, fuil chraorag do chroí
> A' sileadh thar chab mo dháin
> Is an síol a chuiris fadó riamh
> Ag scoilteadh leac an bháis.

> (Celan, see your heart's red blood
> Spurt across this lip of Gaelic verse;
> See the seed you planted then
> Split the mould of death.)

Though life may be, in Dermot Bolger's words, 'a new enslavement' and the Irish scattered to the four corners of the earth, Arthur Cleary survives, Art Ó Laoghaire survives, Paul Celan survives like 'the word (that) comes when needed … its accuracy steadying the heart' (Moya Cannon, 'Taom').

ACKNOWLEDGEMENTS

The following essays first appeared in *Kerry On My Mind: Of Poets, Pedagogues and Place*, Salmon Publishing, Cliffs of Moher, in 1999: 'Poetry and School', 'A Kerry of the Mind', 'My Own Place', 'The Listowel Literary Phenomenon', 'Culpable Innocence?', 'Schooldays', 'Creating the Conscience of the Race: a Portrait of the Artist as a National School Teacher', '"Missing" the Master', 'The Poet in the Classroom', 'The Gift of Ink: The Legacy of Bryan MacMahon', '"Muse, I Claim Your Attention": Celebrating Kerry in Song', 'Approaching Pentecost: Poetry in Contemporary Society', 'Becoming Song: Brendan Kennelly – a Ballylongford of the Heart', 'From Pig-killer to Rain-man: Brendan Kennelly's *The Man Made of Rain*', 'Irish Poetry Now: Other Voices' and 'No Man is an Island'. Grateful acknowledgement is made to Salmon Publishing and to the publisher, my dear friend Jessie Lendennie.

The uncollected essays (they have been slightly altered to suit this collection) first appeared in various books, newspapers and journals. 'Home' (1999), 'Christmas' (1998), 'Up for the Match' (1984), 'Do Chum Glóire Dé agus Onóra na hÉireann' (1999), 'A Kerry Joke: European Funding, *Objective One* Status 1999' (1999), were published in *The Kerryman*. 'Winning isn't Everything' was published in the *North Kerry Senior Football Championship Final Programme 2002*. 'Tread Softly on my Dreams' was published in the *North Kerry Senior Football Championship Final Programme 2003*. 'Up Down!' was published in *Some Old Tales of Clounmacon* in 2000. 'Where History Meets Poetry: Bryan MacMahon and "The Valley of Knockanure"' was published in *The World of Bryan MacMahon* (Mercier Press 2005). '*Sive*: An Introduction' was published in *An Ríocht* in 2003. 'Beating the Goatskin till the Goat Cries: the Importance of Folk Song and Music to John B. Keane, the Man and Playwright' was presented at the first John B. Keane Festival in 2005. 'John B. Keane: A Personal

Perspective' was published in *John B. Keane: Playwright of the People* (North Kerry Literary Trust) in 2004. 'The Passing of an Era' was my oration at the graveside of Con Greaney on 24 June 2001 which was published in part in *The Limerick Leader* and later revised for the *Fleadh Cheoil na hÉireann 2002* programme. 'A Stoic's World: Dennis O'Driscoll's 'Exemplary Damages" was published in *Quadrant* (Australia) in 2003.

'[An] Exile Out Foreign in 'Glantine: Michael Hartnett and the Sense of Place' was delivered as a lecture at Éigse Michael Hartnett in 2001 and published in *Michael Hartnett Remembered* (Four Courts Press 2006). 'Ring Out the Old, Ring in the New' was published in *The Quiet Quarter: Anthology of New Irish Writing* (New Island 2004).

The remainder were broadcast on Lyric FM ('The Quiet Quarter') in 2000: 'That Empty Feeling', 'Sunday Night in Máiréad's Bar, Moyvane', 'Corner Boys', 'Inner Pain' and 'Ring Out the Old, Ring In the New'.

Grateful acknowledgement is made to the following poets, publishers and agents for permission to reproduce copyright material: Garry and Maurice McMahon for works by Bryan MacMahon; the estate of Michael Hartnett and The Gallery Press; Bloodaxe Press for Brendan Kennelly; Criostoir O'Flynn; Desmond Egan; Dermot Bolger; Dennis O'Driscoll; Art Ó Maolfabhail; the estate of Tim Leahy; Patrick Galvin; Moya Cannon; Tomás Mac Síomóin.